Tarla Dalal
India's #1 Cookery Author

1 Teaspoon Cooking with of Oil

Low Calorie Indian Recipes

S&C
SANJAY & CO.
MUMBAI

Fifth Printing : 2005

ISBN : 81-86469-67-2

Price Rs. 250/-

Published & Distributed by : **Sanjay & Company**
353/A-1, Shah & Nahar Industrial Estate, Dhanraj Mill Compound,
Lower Parel (W), Mumbai - 400 013. INDIA.
Tel. : (91-22) 2496 8068 • Fax : (91-22) 2496 5876 • E-mail : sanjay@tarladalal.com

Printed by : **Jupiter Prints**, Mumbai

Recipe Research & Production Design
Pinky Dixit
Arati Fedane
Jyoti Jain

Nutritionists
Nisha Elchiwala
Punam Desai

Marketing Consultant
Harvinder Bindra
Addvalue International

Design
Satyamangal Rege

OTHER BOOKS BY TARLA DALAL

INDIAN COOKING
Tava Cooking
Rotis & Subzis
Desi Khana
The Complete Gujarati Cook Book
Mithai
Chaat
Achaar aur Parathe
The Rajasthani Cookbook
Swadisht Subzian

TOTAL HEALTH
Low Calorie Healthy Cooking
Pregnancy Cookbook
Baby and Toddler Cookbook
Home Remedies
Delicious Diabetic Recipes
Fast Foods Made Healthy
Healthy Soups & Salads
Healthy Breakfast
Calcium Rich Recipes
Healthy Heart Cook Book
Forever Young Diet
Healthy Snacks
Iron Rich Recipes
Healthy Juices New

WESTERN COOKING
The Complete Italian Cookbook
The Chocolate Cookbook
Eggless Desserts
Mocktails & Snacks
Soups & Salads
Mexican Cooking
Easy Gourmet Cooking
Chinese Cooking
Easy Chinese Cooking
Thai Cooking
Sizzlers & Barbeques

MINI SERIES
Idlis & Dosas
Cooking under 10 minutes
Pizzas and Pastas
Fun Food for Children
Roz Ka Khana
Microwave - Desi Khana
T.V. Meals
Paneer
Parathas
Chawal
Dals
Sandwiches
Quick Cooking New

GENERAL COOKING
Exciting Vegetarian Cooking
Microwave Cooking
Quick & Easy Cooking
Saatvik Khana
Mixer Cook Book
The Pleasures of Vegetarian Cooking
The Delights of Vegetarian Cooking
The Joys of Vegetarian Cooking
Cooking With Kids
Snacks Under 10 Minutes
Ice-Cream & Frozen Desserts
Desserts Under 10 Minutes
Entertaining
Microwave Snacks & Desserts

INDEX

1. *Recipe Index* 5
2. *Facts About Oil* 8
    - **a)** Oil, Ghee, Vanaspati or Butter — which one is better? 8
    - **b)** Are 'Oil Free Diets' the Best Option to Lose Weight? 9
    - **c)** How Much Oil Should One Consume Daily? 9
3. *To Lose Weight Correctly and Keep it off Permanently* 10
4. *Eating Healthy and Cooking Healthy go Hand in Hand* 14
5. *Fat Busting Tips* 16
6. *Eating Out* 17
7. *Healthy Dieting Guidelines* 18
8. *Top 8 Diet Questions* 20
9. *Abbreviations Used and Standard Measures* 22
10. *Recipes* 23
11. *Major Nutrients and their Sources* 149
12. *Foods Allowed, Restricted and Forbidden for Weight Watchers* 152
13. *Menu Planner* 157

Introduction

Cooking with 1 teaspoon of oil bids a firm and cheerful goodbye to the widely held notion that delicious Indian food must contain oodles of oil, ghee and butter.

Besides eliminating excessive fat from your daily food, this book will be an indispensable guide for those who wish to lose weight. The common notion about losing weight is to follow a 'zero oil diet' to get rid off the flab. But since experts say that it is a completely unhealthy way to lose weight, I was inspired to write a cookbook especially for weight watchers who constantly crave for delicious and sumptuous foods.

The secret of cooking delectable low fat dishes is learning the art of substitution of foods and by using the right quantum of herbs and spices. For example, trimming fat by using low fat milk instead of full fat milk and cream, using low fat yoghurt as a substitute for mayonnaise to prepare dips and salad dressings (as in the recipe of Chick Pea Salad with Mint Dressing, page 122) etc.

This book also features a vast array of adventurous, nourishing and imaginative Indian recipes, including drinks like Melon Tango, page 38, delicious breakfast ideas like High Fibre Chilas, page 32, wholesome snacks like Moong Dal Seekh Kebabs, page 42, an astounding variety of rotis, subjis and other main meals and guilt-free mouth watering desserts like Low Fat Kulfi with Strawberry Sauce, page 136.

Each recipe in this book has been carefully analysed by a team of qualified nutritionists to ensure that you are getting the correct combination of nutrients throughout the day.

You will find helpful tips and charts explaining the foods that should be eaten and those which should be restricted and avoided along with a menu planner to help you correctly follow a weight loss program. I am sure you will enjoy these easy-to-follow recipes and prepare attractive meals and in addition understand what healthy eating is all about and how to adopt it into your lifestyle.

Happy cooking and healthy eating!

Tarla Dalal

RECIPE INDEX

Delicious Breakfast

1 Muesli 24
2 Nutritious Stuffed Idlis 25
3 Protein Packed Poha 27
4 Mag na Dhokla 28
5 Healthy Breakfast Porridge 29
6 Vegetable Corn Bake 30
7 High Fibre Chilas 32
8 Buckwheat Dhoklas 33

Thirst Quenchers

1 Date and Apple Shake 36
2 Watermelon Slush 37
3 Melon Tango 38
4 Pineapple Celery Juice 39
5 Grape Lassi 40

Wholesome Snacks

1 Moong Dal Seekh Kebabs 42
2 Sprouts Chaat 43
3 Cabbage Jowar Muthias 45
4 Tandoori Mushrooms 47
5 Green Pea Pankis 48
6 Lapsi Methi Muthias 49
7 Swadisht Vegetable Rolls 51
8 Paneer Tikka Kathi Rolls 53

Any Time Munchies

1 Masala Khakhras 56
2 Baked Methi Muthias 59
3 Baked Chaklis 61
4 Low Cal Chivda 62
5 Palak Methi Puris 63

Tongue Tickling Subjis

1	Methi Mutter Pasanda	66
2	Paneer Palak Koftas in Makhani Gravy	68
3	Palak Baby Corn Subji	70
4	Bharva Baingan	71
5	Dahi Bhindi ki Subji	72
6	Healthy Oondhiya	74

Dals and Kadhis

1	Dal Makhani	80
2	Vaal ki Usal	81
3	Kadhai Chole	83
4	Radish Koftas in Kadhi	84
5	Hariyali Dal	86
6	Tamatar ki Kadhi	87
7	Rasam	89
8	Sprouted Kala Chana Ambti	91
9	Turai aur Moong ki Dal	92
10	Sambhar	93
11	Dhan-saak Dal	95

Rice Delicacies

1	Vegetable Biryani	98
2	Masala Bhaat	100
3	Brown Rice	104
4	Spicy Sprouts Pulao	105
5	Lemon Rice	106
6	Soya Mutter Pulao	107

Crispy Rotis and Parathas

1	Methi Makai ki Roti	110
2	Palak aur Chawal ki Roti	111
3	Saatdhan Parathas	112
4	Nutritious Garlic Naans	113
5	Lazeez Parathas	114
6	Methi Paneer Parathas	115
7	Doodhi Theplas	...117
8	Bajra Kand Rotis	...118

Tangy Salads and Raitas

1 Lauki aur Phudine ka Raita 120
2 Barley and Corn Kachumber 121
3 Chick Pea Salad with Mint Dressing 122
4 Pineapple Cucumber Salad 123
5 Crunchy Vegetable Salad 124
6 Spicy Kachumber 125
7 Minty Bean Salad 125
8 Sweet Lime and Pepper Salad 129
9 Mixed Veggie Raita 130

Delectable Mithais

1 Pineapple Basundi 132
2 Sevaiiyan 133
3 Fruit Sandesh 134
4 Low Fat Kulfi with Strawberry Sauce 136
5 Gajar Halwa 138
6 Sweet Potato Puranpoli 139

Basic Recipes

1 Low Fat Milk 142
2 Low Fat Curds 143
3 Low Fat Paneer 144
4 Low Calorie Green Chutney 145
5 Tomato Chutney 146
6 Mint and Coriander Chutney 147

Facts About Oil

Cooking with 1 teaspoon of oil is virtually unthinkable when we speak about Indian food, because large amounts of fats like ghee, cream, butter and oil are used to prepare our daily meals. The use of excessive fat or the wrong kind of fat has been proved to be injurious to health. Parathas, tikkis, kebabs and farsans that feature regularly on our menus contain high amounts of fat.

You'd be surprised to learn that all such recipes that serve 4 portions can be cooked using 1 teaspoon of oil, while retaining their traditional taste and flavour. Our experience with low calorie Indian cooking has been very encouraging and satisfying.

Being trim, fit and healthy doesn't come easy. It requires some determination and commitment to make balanced and healthy eating habits a part of your daily routine. The key to a lifetime of health and fitness is consistency. Here are some suggestions to help you adapt a healthy lifestyle....

a) Oil, Ghee, Vanaspati or Butter — which one is better?

Vegetable oils like olive oil, peanut oil, corn oil, etc. are a healthier option as compared to ghee, vanaspati or butter. This is because oils have a higher proportion of unsaturated fats which do not raise your blood cholesterol levels. In contrast, solid fats like ghee, vanaspati and butter are higher in saturated fats which get converted to cholesterol when consumed. Excessive cholesterol in your blood can lead to clogged arteries and cause heart problems. So using oil in your daily cooking is a better idea but you must carefully choose the oil to stay in good health.

Have small amounts of

- ✔ Olive oil
- ✔ Peanut oil
- ✔ Corn oil
- ✔ Sunflower oil
- ✔ Sesame oil
- ✔ Mustard oil

A combination of the above oils is also healthy as it will provide you with all the essential fatty acids which one kind of oil may lack.

Avoid saturated fats like

- ✔ Ghee
- ✔ Vanaspati
- ✔ Butter
- ✔ Coconut and its products like coconut oil, coconut milk and cream
- ✔ High fat dairy products like full fat milk and milk powder, cream, full fat curds, cheese and full fat paneer (cottage cheese)

b) Are 'Oil Free Diets' the Best Option to Lose Weight?

Although "Oil or Fat Free Diets" may sound betteras they promise to help you knock off weight quickly but it is not a good idea to completely omit oil from your diet. Besides being high in calories (1 gm. of oil or fat = 9 calories), oil contains essential fatty acids which are required to perform certain vital functions in your body. These fatty acids that are provided by oil in your diet cannot be produced naturally by your body. If you do not consume the recommended amount of oil per day, your body becomes deficient in these fatty acids causing visible symptoms like fatigue, weakness, mood swings, dry skin and dry hair. Oil also helps in the absorption of fat-soluble vitamins like vitamins A, D, E and K. Vitamins A and E are important in your daily diet as they antioxidants which help you to build up your immune system to fight against infections. Vitamin D helps in strengthening your bones and teeth whereas vitamin K helps in clotting your blood during injuries.

So be wary of 'zero oil diets', as they can be harmful. The next question that springs to most minds is…

c) How Much Oil Should One Consume Daily?

Oil is a healthier cooking option as compared to saturated fats (ghee, butter etc.) but you need to use it sparingly. It is advisable for healthy individuals to consume no more than 6 teaspoons of oil (30 grams) per day and not more than **3 teaspoons of oil per day** for persons who wish to lose weight. Another way of keeping count is to meassure ½ litre of oil (approx. ½ kg.) per person per month.

To Lose Weight Correctly and Keep it off Permanently

Ensure that your meals are nutritionally well balanced and that you eat adequately each day. Food provides you with energy (expressed as kilocalories or what we commonly refer to as 'calories') which fuels your daily activities. Every adult requires to consume approximately 2000 calories (kilocalories) daily. When you wish to lose weight, you need to reduce the intake by 500 calories each day which means you should follow a **1500-calorie diet.**
Following a low calorie diet doesn't mean eliminating certain foods or cutting out meals. Instead, a diet should be a part of your lifestyle, a way of living, eating the correct way and cultivating habits that will stay with you for a lifetime. A well-balanced diet gives you optimal energy and nutrition for maintenance of your body cells, tissues and organs and supports normal growth and development. Here's what a **balanced diet** *should comprise of,*

a) Carbohydrates

Most of your body's energy (calories or kilocalories) needs should be met by carbohydrates. Ideally 55 to 60 % of your day's total calories should come from complex carbohydrates like cereals, pulses and fibre rich fruits and vegetables (which tend to lower your caloric intake, as they take time to digest and keep you satiated for longer periods). There is a common misconception that a weight watcher's diet must avoid starchy carbohydrate foods like potato, yam etc. as they are considered to be fattening. Yes, they are higher in calories when compared to other vegetables but they provide us with energy and loads of other essential nutrients. Remember that we can make healthy foods fattening by simply adding ghee, butter, cream and rich gravies. For example, carbohydrates rich potatoes are virtually fat free and contain vitamin C, fibre, iron, potassium and some of the B vitamins. Deep frying the same potato to make french fries or chips loads it with only calories. Try a baked potato with veggies instead. However, moderation is the key here too. It is also important to remember that the process of refining decreases the fibre and nutrient content of foods. Hence, it is advisable to avoid refined and processed foods like maida and its products (eg. white bread), canned products etc. Also avoid consuming too much of simple carbohydrates like sugar, aerated drinks etc. which provide you unnecessary calories without any nutritional value. For more carbohydrate rich foods, refer to page 149.

b) Protein

Protein is essential in your diet as it carries out an important function of repair and maintenance of body cells and tissues. A good diet should provide 15 to 20 % of your daily calories from protein.
Pulses, cereals, low fat dairy products are good sources of vegetarian protein and a "must" in your diet. Though non-vegetarian foods are rich in proteins, they are also high in fat so it is best to switch to vegetarian sources.
A combination of cereals and pulses is low in fat and provides you with very good quality of protein which is at par with the non-vegetarian protein. (Refer page 149, to know more about sources of vegetarian protein).
Soyabean and its products (soya nuggets, soya milk, tofu i.e. soya bean curd) should be used more often because they not only are a rich and economical source of high quality vegetarian protein but are also the only source of vitamin B_{12} in a vegetarian diet. Try the recipe of Soya Mutter Pulao on page 107.

c) Fibre

Fibre is very important as it provides you with roughage and also adds bulk to your diet. Dietary fibre keeps you satiated for longer periods of time which in turn reduces the craving for bingeing on high calorie and sugary foods and helps you lose weight. Your daily diet should provide you with at least 15 to 20 grams of fibre.
Whole unprocessed cereals and grains, vegetables and fruits provide you with plenty of fibre when eaten in their natural state. Refined foods like maida and its products do not have fibre and provide you with only calories and should therefore be avoided. Check out the table on page 149, for high fibre foods.

d) Vitamins and Minerals

Have a variety of fruits and vegetables, cooked or raw, as they give you the necessary vitamins and minerals your body needs. For example, papaya and carrot give you vitamin A whereas capsicum and citrus fruits like orange, sweet lime etc. address your vitamin C needs.
Refer to the list given on page 149, to make your fruit and vegetable selection simpler.

Now that you are more acquainted with the nutrients you require, it will be beneficial for you to understand how these nutrients need to be distributed evenly throughout the day. The old saying goes....

'Have breakfast like a king, lunch like a prince and dine like a pauper'.

However, you should not forget the importance of nutritious snacks that often keep you going till the next meal.

Breakfast

Breakfast is a very important meal of your day which weight watchers find easiest to skip to cut down on their calories. The reality is that you have been fasting since dinner and your energy reserves are low in the morning. Begin your day with a high carbohydrate and high fibre breakfast to give you a good start and to keep your energy levels perked up till lunch. A good breakfast keeps you alert and energetic throughout the day. Above all, it keeps you away from bingeing on high calorie mid-morning treats which can lead to unnecessary weight gain.

A balanced breakfast should provide you

- ✔ About 25% of your daily calorie intake
- ✔ A mix of carbohydrates, protein and fibre e.g. Nutritious Stuffed Idlis, page 25 or Muesli, page 24
- ✔ A serving of fruit
- ✔ Plenty of fluids

For some interesting breakfast ideas, refer to page 23.

Lunch

Lunch should be the largest meal of your day after breakfast as your body has time to digest it properly since you are active and on the go. For many of us, a big lunch simply isn't practical, especially on working days. So, choose a lunch that is nutritionally balanced and sustaining enough to keep your energy levels up till the evening. Try out the Hariyali Dal, page 86, with Saatdhan Parathas page 112, along with a wholesome salad. When choosing your lunch, plan ahead about what you're going to have in the evening so you don't double up or miss out on any nutrient.

A balanced lunch should provide you

- ✔ A large proportion of your daily calories
- ✔ A balanced combination of carbohydrates, protein, vitamins, minerals and fat
- ✔ Plenty of fibre which comes from raw salads

Snacking between Meals

When you are on a weight reduction diet, you tend to get hungry faster and so snacks become an increasingly important part of your diet. They add to your overall nutrient intake and must be selected carefully. Include foods like Sprouts Chaat, page 43, fresh fruits, whole wheat bread sandwiches or try some interesting snack options on page 41, when you feel hungry. There is also an entire section on Any Time Munchies, page 55, that you can prepare ahead of time and eat on the run. Select snacks that are low in calories but are nutritionally adequate and tasty enough to tickle your taste buds. Avoid foods like wafers, popcorn, aerated drinks, pastries, chocolates, mithai, white bread etc. which provide you with only unnecessary calories and very few nutrients.

An ideal snack should comprise of a few calories to keep you satiated till your next meal and should provide you

- ✔ A mix of cereals and pulses
- ✔ Vegetables and/or fruits

Dinner

The evening meal is an opportunity to go easy on your calories and eat foods that can be quickly digested. Have more of vegetables, fruits, pulses and unrefined cereals like whole wheat, bajra and jowar. Avoid beans, chick peas and starchy foods (like potatoes and rice) at this time of the day, as these foods take longer to digest and are likely to lead to a restless night if the digestive process is still continuing when you go to bed. Have your dinner as early in the evening as possible. You can always top up with a fresh fruit or a low calorie fruity dessert (like Fruit Sandesh, page 134) later which will provide you vital vitamins and extra fibre. Dry fruit mithais and halwas are indulgences which are all high in sugar and fat and so are best avoided.

A balanced dinner should provide you

- ✔ Fewer calories as compared to lunch but enough to keep you satiated through the night
- ✔ Fibre by way of a salad or a fruit

Eating Healthy and Cooking Healthy go Hand in Hand...

A healthy balanced diet isn't just about eating the right kind of food. The way that you buy, store, prepare and cook your food and even the pots, pans and equipment you use, all have a significant impact on the nutritional value of the foods you eat.

Buy the freshest. Buy only the freshest fruits and vegetables available in the market. Seasonal fruits are the most nutritious as they ripen without the usage of additional chemicals and are more reasonably priced.

Eat fresh. Refrigerating food for long periods results in the loss of vital nutrients. So buy in small quantities and cook for the day! Also try and avoid storing left-over food as re-heating it results in nutrient loss.

Eat veggies and fruits with their skin on. As far as possible, eat vegetables and fruits unpeeled so that you don't lose out on fibre and nutrients. Vegetables and fruits like cucumber, potatoes, carrots, apple, chickoo etc. have vital nutrients right under the peel which you lose out on if you peel them. Remember to scrub these vegetables and fruits thoroughly before you eat them as they may contain a thin film of mud and pesticides.

Eat more sprouts. Sprouts are remarkable foods, cheap and nutritious. The process of sprouting induces a frenzy of biochemical changes in which complex substances break down to simpler forms which makes them easier to digest. Sprouted legumes also have higher vitamin C, iron and calcium levels than those legumes which are not sprouted.

Try some delicious recipes using sprouts like Sprouted Kala Chana Ambti, page 91, and Spicy Sprouts Pulao, page 105, among others. So, here's to happy sprouting!!

Steam and sauté rather than boil. Carefully cook vegetables so that they retain most of their nutrients during the cooking process. Therefore, it is better to sauté or steam vegetables rather than to boil them. If you do boil the vegetables, use minimum quantity of water and cook only until the vegetables become tender. Use a pressure cooker to cook vegetables as pressure cooking requires less oil and also helps to conserve the volatile nutrients like vitamins B and C.

Save nutrients. Do not throw away the water in which dals, rice and veggies have been cooked, as it contains water-soluble nutrients such as vitamin B and C that are released during cooking. It is advisable to add just enough quantity of water and cover foods while cooking to preserve the volatile nutrients. Any excess cooking water that is remaining can be used to make soups or to knead your chapati dough, as this is a good way to use the water-soluble vitamins. Whenever possible, cook food in large pieces as vegetables cut into small pieces lose more nutrients.

Fat Busting Tips

When you are fighting the battle of bulge, it is certainly desirable to avoid saturated fats and to use oil in your daily cooking. At the same time, also try to reduce all other forms of fat from your diet. So…

- Always use oil sparingly when cooking. If a recipe calls for 1 teaspoon of oil, measure it rather than guessing.
- Use non-stick cookware with lids to reduce the amount of oil being used for cooking.
- When using 1 teaspoon of oil for cooking for 4 portions in recipes, the tempering tends to burn more quickly. Do not get tempted to add more oil. Instead, add some water.
- We normally cook vegetables in oil. It is a better idea to steam your veggies first, before adding them into gravies.
- Instead of coconut and dry fruits, use vegetable pureés in gravies as in the recipe of Paneer Palak Koftas in Makhani Gravy, page 68.
- Choose baking instead of deep frying wherever possible. Baked Palak Methi Puris, page 64, are an excellent example of this cooking method.
- Replace full fat dairy products with low fat alternatives like low fat milk, milk powder, curds and paneer.
- Use low fat salad dressings instead of mayonnaise and salad cream. Try the recipe of Chick Pea Salad with Mint Dressing, page 122.
- Stop snacking on peanuts, almonds and other nuts as these have plenty of hidden fats.
- Read food labels carefully, particularly those claiming to be low fat foods. Low fat products may still contain more fat than you think.
- Beware of high fat products like cakes, pastries, all types of mithais and savouries, sweet and savoury biscuits, chocolates, all types of instant soups, sauces, popcorn with butter and excess oil etc.

Eating Out

Dining out doesn't have to be a caloric catastrophe. Learn how to order with your waistline in mind.

Do....

- Select foods that are low in fat and sugar.
- Choose an unsweetened fruit juice or lassi instead of aerated beverages.
- Order a salad with low fat dressing as it's the oil-laden dressings that make salads unhealthy. Choose a lemon or low fat curd dressing instead of a high calorie mayonnaise or cream based dressing.
- Choose a whole wheat roti instead of white bread or naan made out of maida. Maida (refined flour) provides very little nutrition and virtually no fibre.
- Select stir-fried vegetables which use less oil while cooking instead of greasy calorie-laden gravies.
- If you really crave for desserts, select a less fatty, fruit based dessert and share it with someone, so that you don't feel obligated to finish the entire portion.

Not to do...

- Avoid eating out too often. Let it be an occasional indulgence.
- Never arrive at a restaurant on an empty stomach. This is beacause most restaurant dinners tend to start off late and if you are really hungry, you may end up bingeing on fried starters or calorie-laden food. To avoid this, have a small snack or a piece of fruit before you leave home.
- Avoid an alcoholic drink before or after dinner as it provides you with only empty (unnecessary) calories.
- Avoid butter and cheese-laden dishes like pav bhaji, sandwiches, butter idlis and dosas.
- Don't overeat just because you do not want to waste the food you have ordered. Pack the leftovers so you can relish them later when you're hungry or you can give it to someone on your way home.

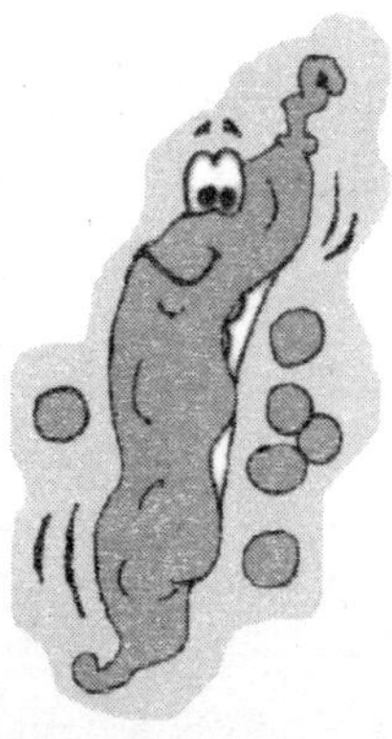

Healthy Dieting Guidelines

For those who really wish to lose weight, it helps even if they can make small but significant changes in their daily life. One doesn't necessarily have to go on a stringent diet. . .just being aware of what you are eating helps a lot! You must. . .

Make changes gradually. Don't try to do everything at once. It will take longer to lose weight when you are following a correct weight loss plan, but you will be able to keep the weight off permanently.

Always set a realistic target to lose weight. It is always better to lose weight gradually rather than drastically. A drastic weight loss program results in loss of water and precious tissues from your body instead of fat. Aim to **lose ½ kg every week** and not a drastic 5 kgs a week. Walk two blocks at first, not 2 miles. Success will come more easily and you will be motivated to continue!

Do not eat your meals in a hurry. No matter how packed your schedule is, don't get tempted to grab a sandwich and eat on the run. Your body will absorb more nutrients if you take the time to sit down, relax and enjoy your meals. Resting quietly for 5 or 10 minutes afterwards will give your body an opportunity to digest.

Do not skip your meals, as you will be tempted to binge on high calorie snacks and end up putting on weight rather than losing it. Eat your meals regularly!

Listen to your hunger pangs. Most of the times we tend to overeat without realizing how hungry we are. It is always better to chew your food properly, as chewing helps in better digestion and also gives you enough time to know how hungry you are and when you have reached your satiation levels.

Don't reach out for second helpings. Serve yourself at one time, sit down and relish your meal. That's the best way to reduce temptations and monitor how much you eat.

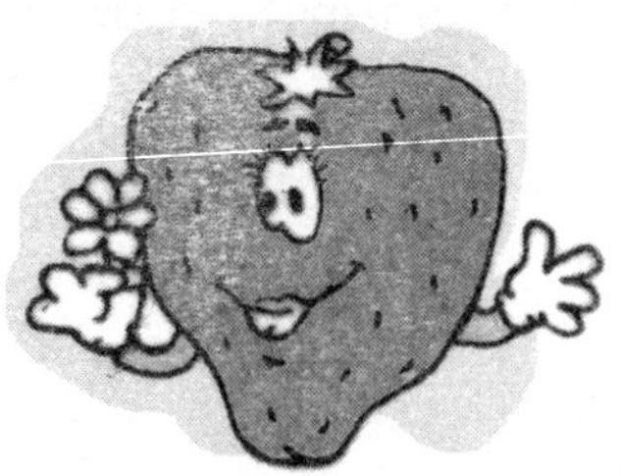

Drink plenty of fluids. Having a glass of water before meals helps you cut down on your food intake. You tend to eat less when you drink more fluids and end up losing weight. If you get bored of drinking plain water, feel free to squeeze a lemon into it. Drink plenty of water, unsweetened juices and coconut water everyday. You should have at least 8 to 10 glasses of water each day. But try and stay off caffeinated beverages like tea, coffee etc. as they interfere with the absorption of nutrients in your body. Also the sugar added to prepare tea and coffee provides you with nothing but empty calories.

Plan your weekly menu. Always plan your meals, preferably for a week so that you don't cook or buy any impulse high calorie foods.

Record everything you eat in a book. It will help you track the foods consumed in a day and also to keep tab on your daily calories.

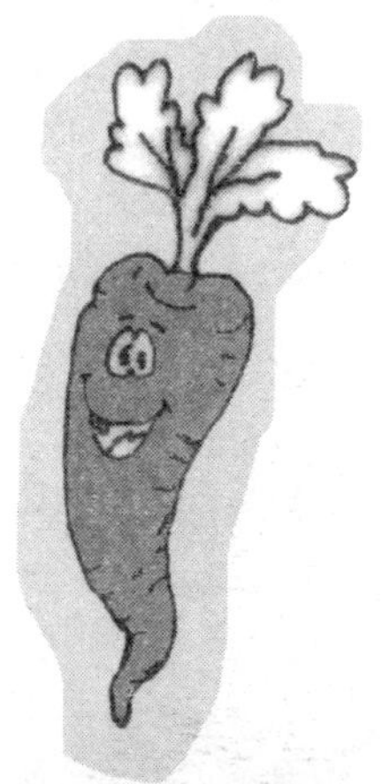

Exercise. If you combine a healthy diet with exercise, you will increase your body's metabolic rate, burn a lot more calories from fat and lose weight quickly. Exercise increases your good cholesterol — HDL (high density lipoprotein), decreases bad cholesterol — LDL (low density lipoprotein) and prevents heart diseases. It also improves your health and will drive away fatigue. To increase your overall activity levels...

a) run up the stairs instead of using the lift

b) walk short distances instead of taking a cab

c) set aside time for regular exercise (like aerobics, swimming etc.) at least 4 days a week for a minimum span of 30 minutes each time.

Exercise will not only improve your body shape and tone your muscles but will also improve your mental well being.

Reward yourself. When you achieve your short term weight loss goal, do something special for yourself. Go for a movie, buy a new shirt, read a book, visit a friend and pamper yourself.

Top 8 Diet Questions

1 Why should you avoid Crash or Fad diets?

There is nothing magical about fad diets. Their secret involves a significant and drastic reduction in calories. People following these diets are basically starving themselves by eating watery soups and vegetables. They can't help but lose a lot of water weight and not fat. Crash or fad diets severely limit food choices or are unbalanced in some way. For example, only boiled vegetables or sprouts are suggested eliminating all other food choices.

Since, fad diets do nothing to change long term eating habits, most fad dieters' gain back more weight than they lost as soon as they go back to their old ways of eating.

2 What is invisible fat?

This is the hidden fat present in all foods in varying amounts. For example, nuts and oilseeds like peanuts, sesame seeds etc. contain plenty of invisible fat as compared to vegetables which contain small amounts of it whereas cereals and pulses contain moderate amounts of invisible fat. To put it simply, you get 26 grams of invisible fat from 100 grams of peanuts in comparison 100 grams of spinach contains only 0.7 grams of invisible fat. If you are on a weight loss program, it is important to remember that these can add on to the total fat (and calories) consumed in a day.

3 Sugar, jaggery or honey—which one is better?

Sugar, jaggery or honey provide you approximately the same amount of calories (20 calories per teaspoon) and no appreciable amounts of other nutrients. It is better to use jaggery for recipes (but restrict the quantities) as compared to sugar and honey, as it is a good source of iron. You don't have to go on a sugar eliminating diet to lose weight but it is a good idea to cut down on sugar and to satisfy your sweet cravings by eating small portions of a low calorie dessert or a piece of fruit instead.

4 What are empty calories?

Calories obtained from foods that are completely void of nutrients are called "empty calories". Aerated drinks, refined sugar and alcohol are foods that provide you only calories (empty calories) which could lead to weight gain, as all excess calories are converted into fat and stored in your body. So, it is best to avoid these foods to effectively lose weight.

5 Are fruits healthier than their juices?

Yes, fruits are healthier than their juices because the process of extracting juice removes all the fibre present in the fruit. Fibre is essential as it aids digestion, relieves constipation and lowers blood cholesterol levels. It adds bulk to your diet and keeps you satiated for a longer period of time. If a glass of fruit juice is what you want to have, do not strain fruit juice so as to retain its fibre. Also resist the temptation to sweeten the juice with sugar to avoid loading it with empty calories. Refer to the recipe of Pineapple Celery Juice, page 39.

6 Rice or wheat—which one is healthier?

Whole wheat is richer in fibre than the polished rice we are used to consuming. Rice has approximately the same calories as whole wheat and hence is not more fattening. But the kind of rice you choose is of utmost importance. Brown rice (unpolished rice) abounds in fibre which aids in digestion while helping to lower your blood cholesterol levels whereas white rice (polished rice) loses this important nutrient (i.e. fibre) during processing. If you don't like the taste of brown rice, it is wiser to opt for whole wheat or to eat small portions of white rice with large servings of vegetables (as they are rich in fibre). Alternatively, a one-meal combination of rice cooked with plenty of vegetables, like in the recipe of Vegetable Biryani, page 98, is also a healthy option.

7 Do you need to eliminate dairy products, if you wish to lose weight?

No you don't need to eliminate dairy products when you are on a reducing diet, as they are the biggest source of calcium that is essential for healthy bones and teeth. They also provide substantial amounts of protein and vitamins A and B. But you should replace high fat dairy products (like full fat milk, milk powder, curds and paneer etc.) with their low fat alternatives (skim or low fat milk and milk products) when you aim to lose weight.

Low fat dairy products are equally good sources of the above nutrients, with fewer calories and traces of fat. However, you do need to skip dairy foods like cheese, cream and butter, as these are very high in fat.

8 Are soups and salads always low in calories?

It is true that soups and salads are nourishing as they make use of a wide variety of vegetables, fresh fruits and sprouts but we often make them unhealthy by using salad dressings like mayonnaise and by loading soups with butter, cream, cheese etc. These ingredients are very high in calories, fat and cholesterol and do no good to your body. Rather they increase your weight. Instead, you should make use of flavourful herbs and spices to prepare delectable soups and salads which are healthy, tasty and low in calories.

Besides the dietary guidelines I've discussed above, high-self esteem is equally important to maintain a healthy, balanced lifestyle and it's a must if successful weight loss is one of your goals. What's more important is that you feel good about who you are and how you look rather than setting unrealistic weight loss targets. Learn to love your body and put yourself in a more positive light. So stop starving and do not junk your body by eating fast foods. Instead, let's get introduced to our vast repertoire of ingredients, herbs and spices and reacquaint ourselves with fresh vegetables and fruits and cook them correctly using 1 teaspoon of oil.
And I bet you'll end up feeling really good and lose weight too…

Abbreviations Used

The table below lists the abbreviations used in this book:

CHO	Carbohydrates
F.ACID	Folic acid
VIT.A	Vitamin A
VIT.C	Vitamin C
AMT	Amount
gm	Grams
kcal	Kilocalories
kg	Kilograms
mcg	Micrograms
mg	Milligrams
ml	Millilitres

Standard Measures

All recipes and nutritional values are based on standard cup and spoon measures. They are:

1 cup = 200 ml.
1 tablespoon = 15 ml.
1 teaspoon = 5 ml.

Delicious Breakfast

Muesli

Picture on page 57

Preparation time :
5 minutes.

Cooking time :
10 minutes.

Serves 4.

A powerhouse to start the day. All the ingredients for this recipe can be very easily put together and you can relish the taste of each ingredient in the final product. This protein packed dish is loaded with carbohydrates, fibre and calcium besides minerals like iron and folic acid. You can store this muesli for several days in an air-tight container and prepare a healthy breakfast in a jiffy by just adding warm milk and apples.

2 cups cornflakes
1 cup quick rolled cooking oats
4 tablespoons wheat bran
¼ teaspoon vanilla essence
3 tablespoons sultanas (kismis)

For serving

4 cups of warm low fat milk, page 142
1 apple (unpeeled), chopped

1. Combine the oats and wheat bran and lightly roast them in a non-stick pan over a slow flame for 5 to 7 minutes.
2. Cool completely, add the cornflakes, vanilla essence and sultanas. Mix well. Store in an air-tight container.
3. For serving, place the muesli into individual bowls with the apple and pour warm milk.
   Serve immediately.

Nutritive values per serving :

AMT	ENERGY	PROTEIN	CHO	FAT	VIT.A	VIT.C	CALCIUM	IRON	F.ACID	FIBRE
gm	kcal	gm	gm	gm	mcg	mg	mg	mg	mcg	gm
123	281	13.2	51.6	2.3	0.4	1.6	308.9	3.9	38.2	2.6

Nutritious Stuffed Idlis

Preparation time :
10 minutes.

Cooking time :
20 minutes.

Makes 15 idlis.

Even though idlis are nourishing breakfast foods, the accompanying coconut chutney adds on extra calories and fat. So here's a colourful idli recipe that's packed with the goodness of vegetables and served with delicious low calorie green chutney made without using coconut, for healthy and delicious eating!

For the idli batter

1 cup rice semolina (idli rawa)
¼ cup poha (beaten rice flakes)
¼ cup urad dal (split black lentils)
salt to taste

For the stuffing

2 cups mixed vegetables (carrots, peas, french beans), diced
2 green chillies, finely chopped
5 to 6 curry leaves
½ teaspoon urad dal (split black lentils)
½ teaspoon mustard seeds (rai)
1 teaspoon oil
salt to taste

Other ingredients

oil for greasing

For serving

sambhar, page 93 or low calorie green chutney, page 145

1. Wash and soak the rice semolina and poha in water for at least 2 hours.
2. Wash the urad dal thoroughly and soak it in water for at least 2 hours.

3. Blend the rice semolina and poha in a blender to make a smooth batter.
4. Grind the urad dal separately to a smooth paste using a little water.
5. Mix the two batters and add salt. Cover and keep aside for 6 to 8 hours for fermenting.

For the stuffing

1. Coarsely grind the mixed vegetables in a blender without using any water.
2. Heat the oil in a non-stick pan, add the green chillies, curry leaves, urad dal and mustard seeds and sauté for a few seconds.
3. When the seeds crackle, add the vegetables and salt and sauté for 3 to 4 minutes. Divide the stuffing into 15 equal portions. Keep aside.

How to proceed

1. Place a spoonful of the idli batter into each greased idli mould.
2. Place a portion of the stuffing over the idli batter.
3. Pour a spoonful of idli batter to cover the stuffing on each idli mould.
4. Steam for 10 to 12 minutes. Wait for 1 minute and take out the idlis. Serve hot, with sambhar or low calorie green chutney.

Nutritive values per idli :

AMT	ENERGY	PROTEIN	CHO	FAT	VIT.A	VIT.C	CALCIUM	IRON	F.ACID	FIBRE
gm	kcal	gm	gm	gm	mcg	mg	mg	mg	mcg	gm
29	65	2.0	13.3	0.4	61.5	1.7	10.8	0.6	7.8	0.4

Protein Packed Poha

Preparation time :
10 minutes.
Cooking time :
10 minutes.
Serves 4.

A nutritious breakfast taken early in the morning holds you in good stead throughout the day. Batata poha is a breakfast dish that's really easy to make and is commonly eaten in most houses. To make it healthier, I have substituted potatoes with sprouts in this recipe as sprouted pulses are easier to digest while providing precious nutrients like iron, calcium and vitamins B and C.

1½ cups jada poha (beaten rice flakes)
1½ cups mixed sprouts (moath beans, moong, red chana etc.), boiled
½ teaspoon mustard seeds (rai)
1 large onion, finely chopped
1 to 2 green chillies, chopped
¼ teaspoon turmeric powder (haldi)
2 teaspoons sugar
3 teaspoons lemon juice
1 teaspoon oil
salt to taste

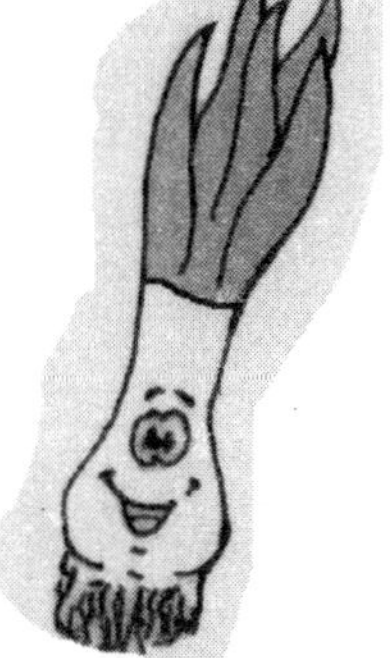

For the garnish
2 tablespoons chopped coriander

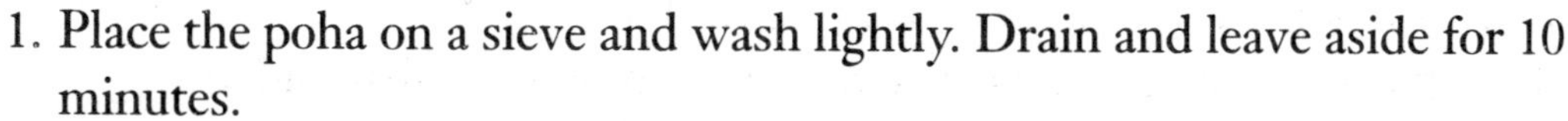

1. Place the poha on a sieve and wash lightly. Drain and leave aside for 10 minutes.
2. Heat the oil in a non-stick pan and add the mustard seeds. When they crackle, add the onion and green chillies and sauté till the onion turns translucent.
3. Add the mixed sprouts, turmeric powder, sugar and salt with approx. ½ cup of water and sauté for 3 to 4 minutes.
4. Add the poha and lemon juice and mix well.
   Serve hot, garnished with the coriander.

Nutritive values per serving :

AMT	ENERGY	PROTEIN	CHO	FAT	VIT.A	VIT.C	CALCIUM	IRON	F.ACID	FIBRE
gm	kcal	gm	gm	gm	mcg	mg	mg	mg	mcg	gm
76	156	4.8	30.3	3.1	151.4	9.5	43.6	5.4	1.5	1.1

Mag na Dhokla

Moong or 'mag na' dhoklas are a favourite breakfast recipe of Gujaratis. Not only are these dhoklas very simple to prepare but they can also be made well in advance. To enhance the flavour and nutritive value, add some grated carrots or ground peas to the batter.
Serve with Low Calorie Green Chutney, page 145.

Preparation time :
10 minutes.
Cooking time :
25 minutes.
Serves 4.

1½ cups whole green moong (whole green gram)
2 teaspoons ginger-green chilli paste
1 teaspoon cumin seed (jeera) powder
1 cup low fat curds, page 143
1½ teaspoons Eno's fruit salt
salt to taste

For the garnish
2 tablespoons chopped coriander

1. Soak the moong for 4 hours. Drain and grind to a coarse paste.
2. Add the ginger-green chilli paste, cumin seed powder, curds and salt.
3. Grease a 200 mm. (8") diameter thali and keep aside.
4. Divide the batter into 2 parts.
5. Add ¾ teaspoon of the fruit salt to half of the batter. Mix well, pour into the greased thali and steam immediately for 10 to 12 minutes.
6. Repeat step 5 for the remaining half of the batter.
7. Cool slightly and cut into diamond shaped pieces.
   Serve, garnished with the coriander.

Handy Tip *It is important to add the fruit salt just before you put the dhoklas to steam.*

Nutritive values per serving :

AMT	ENERGY	PROTEIN	CHO	FAT	VIT.A	VIT.C	CALCIUM	IRON	F.ACID	FIBRE
gm	kcal	gm	gm	gm	mcg	mg	mg	mg	mcg	gm
72	246	17.9	41.7	0.8	135.7	2.3	120.2	2.6	91.4	0.5

Healthy Breakfast Porridge

Preparation time :
15 minutes.
Cooking time :
20 minutes.
Serves 4.

If you're bored of the regular breakfast dishes, try this new healthy recipe made using jowar. Jowar is a nutritious cereal with plenty of protein, iron and fibre. The curds and vegetables improve its vitamin A and calcium levels.
This vegetable porridge accompanied by a fruit is sure to keep you satiated till lunch and prevent you from bingeing on unhealthy mid-morning snacks like biscuits, nuts, chips etc.

½ cup jowar (white millet)
1 cup mixed chopped vegetables (carrots, green peas, french beans)
½ teaspoon mustard seeds (rai)
a pinch asafoetida (hing)
1 teaspoon oil
salt to taste

2 tablespoons chopped tomato
2 tablespoons chopped onion
2 teaspoons chopped coriander

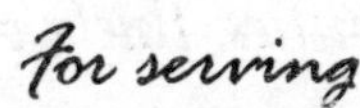

1 cup fresh low fat curds, page 143

1. Grind the jowar to a coarse powder in a blender.
2. Combine the ground jowar and salt with 3 cups of water and pressure cook for 3 to 4 whistles or till it is cooked.
3. Heat the oil in a non-stick pan and add the mustard seeds and asafoetida.
4. When the seeds crackle, add the vegetables and sauté for 4 to 5 minutes.
5. Add the cooked jowar mixture with 1½ cups of water and simmer for 7 to 8 minutes.
6. Top with the tomato, onion and coriander.
   Serve hot, with curds.

Handy Tip *If the porridge becomes too thick while serving, adjust its consistency by adding some water.*

Nutritive values per serving :

AMT	ENERGY	PROTEIN	CHO	FAT	VIT.A	VIT.C	CALCIUM	IRON	F.ACID	FIBRE
gm	kcal	gm	gm	gm	mcg	mg	mg	mg	mcg	gm
64	120	5.2	21.0	1.7	251.0	7.7	92.1	1.3	11.7	1.1

Vegetable Corn Bake

Preparation time :
15 minutes.
Baking time :
50 minutes.
Baking temperature :
180°C (360°F).
Serves 4.

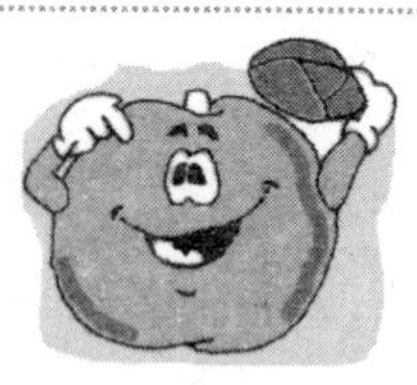

This delicious corn recipe is a great way to begin your day. It is really low in calories and vegetables add bulk and vitamins while fresh ginger and chilli add pungent accents to this treat. Serve hot, with Mint and Coriander Chutney, page 147.

2 sweet corn cobs, grated
1½ cups cabbage, grated
½ cup bottle gourd (doodhi / lauki), grated
½ cup Bengal gram flour (besan)
2 teaspoons ginger paste
1 to 2 green chillies, finely chopped

½ cup chopped coriander
2 teaspoons sugar
2 tablespoons lemon juice
a pinch soda bi-carb
salt to taste
oil for greasing

For the tempering

1 teaspoon oil
½ teaspoon mustard seeds (rai)
a pinch asafoetida (hing)

For serving

mint and coriander chutney, page 147

1. Combine all the ingredients in a bowl and mix well. Transfer into a greased 150 mm. (6") diameter baking dish.
2. For the tempering, heat the oil in a pan and add the mustard seeds and asafoetida. When the seeds crackle, pour the tempering over the mixture in the baking dish.
3. Bake in a pre-heated oven at 180°C (360°F) for 40 to 50 minutes or till the centre is firm.

   Serve hot, with mint and coriander chutney.

Nutritive values per serving :

AMT	ENERGY	PROTEIN	CHO	FAT	VIT.A	VIT.C	CALCIUM	IRON	F.ACID	FIBRE
gm	kcal	gm	gm	gm	mcg	mg	mg	mg	mcg	gm
174	203	7.6	36.5	2.9	300.6	54.1	45.1	2.0	22.2	1.6

High Fibre Chilas

Preparation time :
2 hours.

Cooking time :
15 minutes.

Makes 4 chilas.

Scrumptious pancakes made using buckwheat which is extremely high in fibre and iron. Carrot and spring onions add crunch to these soft pancakes, apart from providing substantial amounts of vitamin A.
When served with Low Calorie Green Chutney, page 145, they are sure to bring a smile on your face.

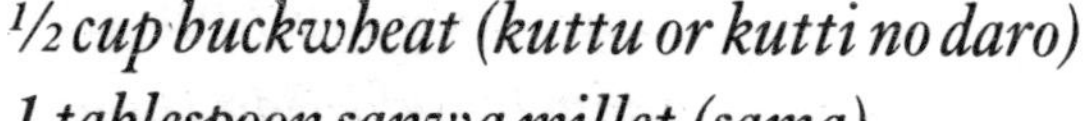

½ cup buckwheat (kuttu or kutti no daro)
1 tablespoon sanwa millet (sama)
¼ cup low fat curds, page 143
1 teaspoon ginger-green chilli paste
⅔ cup grated carrot
⅔ cup chopped spring onions (including greens)
1 tablespoon chopped coriander
salt to taste

Other ingredients

1 teaspoon oil for cooking

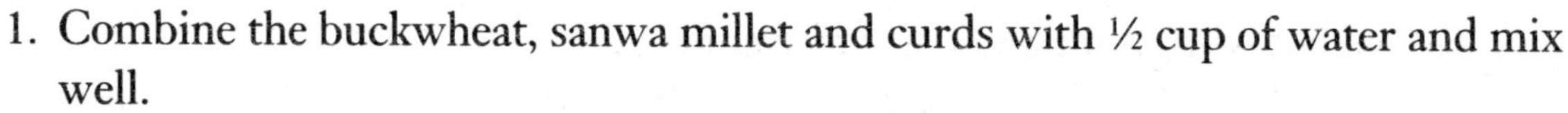

1. Combine the buckwheat, sanwa millet and curds with ½ cup of water and mix well.
2. Allow it to soak for 2 hours.
3. Liquidise this mixture in a blender till it is a smooth purée.
4. Pour it into a bowl and add the ginger-green chilli paste, carrot, spring onions, coriander and salt and mix well.
5. Pour approx. 3 tablespoons of this batter onto a heated non-stick pan. Cook the chila on both sides using a little oil, till both sides are golden brown.
6. Repeat with the remaining batter to make 3 more chilas.

Variation : *You can also make these chilas without adding the carrot and spring onions.*

Nutritive values per chila :

AMT	ENERGY	PROTEIN	CHO	FAT	VIT.A	VIT.C	CALCIUM	IRON	F.ACID	FIBRE
gm	kcal	gm	gm	gm	mcg	mg	mg	mg	mcg	gm
49	94	2.7	16.8	1.8	375.0	2.6	47.7	3.1	3.0	2.1

Buckwheat Dhoklas

Preparation time :
3 hours.
Cooking time :
20 minutes.
Serves 4.

This combination of buckwheat, sanwa millet and curds makes an interesting recipe which is best enjoyed when served piping hot with a spoonful of Low Calorie Green Chutney, page 145.

I've selected buckwheat as it abounds in fibre that will keep you satiated for a longer time and will prevent you from munching on calorie-laden snacks. Curds give a smooth creamy texture to the dhokla batter while enriching it with calcium which is necessary for healthy and strong bones.

You can also have these dhoklas when you're on a religious fast as both these ingredients can be consumed during fasts.

1 cup buckwheat (kutto or kutti no daro)
2 tablespoons sanwa millet (sama)
3/4 cup fresh low fat curds, page 143
1 teaspoon ginger-green chilli paste
1 teaspoon oil
a pinch soda bi-carb
salt to taste

Other ingredients

oil for greasing

For the garnish

1 tablespoon chopped coriander

1. Wash and drain the buckwheat. Add the sanwa millet and curds and mix well. Allow to soak for at least 3 hours.
2. Add the ginger-green chilli paste, oil, soda bi-carb and salt and mix well.
3. Pour the batter into a 200 mm. (8") diameter greased thali.
4. Steam for 12 to 15 minutes till the dhoklas are firm.
5. Cool slightly and cut into diamond shaped pieces.
   Serve hot, garnished with the coriander.

Nutritive values per serving :

AMT	ENERGY	PROTEIN	CHO	FAT	VIT.A	VIT.C	CALCIUM	IRON	F.ACID	FIBRE
gm	kcal	gm	gm	gm	mcg	mg	mg	mg	mcg	gm
46	156	5.4	28.6	2.2	11.3	0.2	75.0	5.8	0.0	3.6

Thirst Quenchers

Date and Apple Shake

Preparation time :
20 minutes.

Cooking time :
2 minutes.

Makes 4 glasses.

All of us are aware of the famous proverb "An apple a day keeps a doctor away". So here's a perfect fat and natural sugar drink made of apples blended with dates and milk to start off your day. Chill all the ingredients before making the shake. Also remember to finish it quickly, as the apples tend to discolour very quickly.

4 cups low fat milk, page 142
1 large apple, chopped
10 black dates, deseeded and finely chopped
a few drops vanilla essence
3 to 4 ice-cubes

1. Soak the dates in ½ cup of warm milk and leave aside for at least 20 minutes.
2. Blend all the ingredients in a liquidiser and pour into 4 individual glasses. Serve chilled.

Nutritive values per glass :

AMT	ENERGY	PROTEIN	CHO	FAT	VIT.A	VIT.C	CALCIUM	IRON	F.ACID	FIBRE
gm	kcal	gm	gm	gm	mcg	mg	mg	mg	mcg	gm
85	120	7.9	21.5	0.3	0.0	1.5	282.0	0.7	0.0	1.0

Watermelon Slush *Picture on cover*

Preparation time :
5 minutes.
No Cooking.
Serves 2.

Watermelons are ideal for those on a low calorie diet as more than 75% of the fruit consists of water and it is really low in calories (1 cup = 25 calories). The fruit also contains appreciable amounts of protein and iron.
It's a great cooler for warm afternoons.

3 cups watermelon, cut into small pieces
¼ teaspoon roasted cumin seeds (jeera) powder
1 teaspoon sugar
¼ teaspoon black salt (sanchal)
3 tablespoons low fat milk, page 142

1. Blend the watermelon pieces in a liquidiser to a smooth purée.
2. Combine all the ingredients in a bowl and mix well.
3. Pour the mixture into a shallow freezer proof container and freeze until it is firm (approx. 2 hours).
4. Blend the mixture in a liquidiser till it is slushy.
5. Pour into 2 glasses and serve immediately.

Nutritive values per glass :

AMT	ENERGY	PROTEIN	CHO	FAT	VIT.A	VIT.C	CALCIUM	IRON	F.ACID	FIBRE
gm	kcal	gm	gm	gm	mcg	mg	mg	mg	mcg	gm
242	55	1.2	11.	0.5	0.0	2.5	51.8	18.7	0.0	0.5

Melon Tango

Picture on page 57

Preparation time :
5 minutes.

No Cooking.

Serves 4.

The unusual combination of muskmelon, orange and coconut water lends a refreshing flavour to this drink. This vitamin C loaded fruity concoction has been an all-time favourite amongst my family and friends. A touch of black salt perks it up, but you can also do without it, if you prefer.

2 cups muskmelon (kharbooja), cubed
juice of 2 oranges
2 cups tender coconut water
2 teaspoons sugar
a pinch black salt (sanchal)

For the garnish

a few mint leaves

1. Blend the melon in a liquidiser and strain it.
2. Combine all the ingredients and mix well.

Serve chilled, poured into glasses and garnished with mint leaves.

Handy Tips

1. To reduce the amount of sugar required, use a ripe muskmelon.
2. You can even make this juice without straining the muskmelon.

Nutritive values per serving :

AMT	ENERGY	PROTEIN	CHO	FAT	VIT.A	VIT.C	CALCIUM	IRON	F.ACID	FIBRE
gm	kcal	gm	gm	gm	mcg	mg	mg	mg	mcg	gm
266	89	2.2	19.1	0.4	1098.3	47.9	70.9	1.4	0.0	0.6

Pineapple Celery Juice

Picture on page 75

Preparation time : 15 minutes.

No Cooking.

Makes 4 glasses.

A fibre laden drink made with pineapple and celery, which is pepped up by a touch of black salt. Pineapple has loads of iron and also vitamin C (which aids in the absorption of iron in your body). Celery adds vitamin A to this cooling drink which is a perfect hot summer treat.

4 cups ripe pineapple, cut into small pieces
4 tablespoons celery, finely chopped
1 teaspoon black salt (sanchal)

1. Combine the pineapple and celery with 2 cups of water and liquidise till it becomes a purée.
2. Add the black salt and mix well.
   Serve immediately.

Nutritive values per glass :

AMT	ENERGY	PROTEIN	CHO	FAT	VIT.A	VIT.C	CALCIUM	IRON	F.ACID	FIBRE
gm	kcal	gm	gm	gm	mcg	mg	mg	mg	mcg	gm
178	79	0.8	18.3	0.2	92.3	65.5	60.8	4.6	0.0	1.0

Grape Lassi

Preparation time : 5 minutes.

No Cooking.

Makes 4 glasses.

Black grapes blend very well with curds and also provide lots of fibre.

Lassi is an excellent thirst quencher during the summers. Remember to use fresh low fat curds and really sweet grapes for this referesbing drink.

2 cups black grapes
1 cup fresh low fat curds, page 143
1 cup low fat milk, page 142
4 teaspoons sugar
ice -cubes to serve

1. Combine all the ingredients and blend in a liquidiser.
2. Pour into individual glasses, top with ice-cubes and serve chilled.

Nutritive values per glass :

AMT	ENERGY	PROTEIN	CHO	FAT	VIT.A	VIT.C	CALCIUM	IRON	F.ACID	FIBRE
gm	kcal	gm	gm	gm	mcg	mg	mg	mg	mcg	gm
85	105	4.2	21.6	0.2	0.0	1.2	151.0	0.5	0.0	2.0

Wholesome Snacks

Moong Dal Seekh Kebabs

Preparation time :
10 minutes.

Cooking time :
25 minutes.

Makes 12 kebabs.

This is a vegetarian version of the non-vegetarian seekh kebabs.
Moong dal when combined with potatoes and onions tastes simply superb besides providing protein which is required for the healthy maintenance of your body cells. Dip these kebabs in your favourite sauce or chutney. Alternatively, serve them wrapped in rotis to make kebab rolls, a more filling snack.

½ cup yellow moong dal (split yellow gram)
¼ cup boiled potato, grated
2 tablespoons grated onion
2 teaspoons chilli powder
¼ teaspoon garam masala
¼ teaspoon turmeric powder (haldi)
½ teaspoon ginger-garlic paste
2 teaspoons chaat masala
2 tablespoons chopped coriander
salt to taste

Other ingredients
1 teaspoon oil for cooking

For serving
mint and coriander chutney, page 147

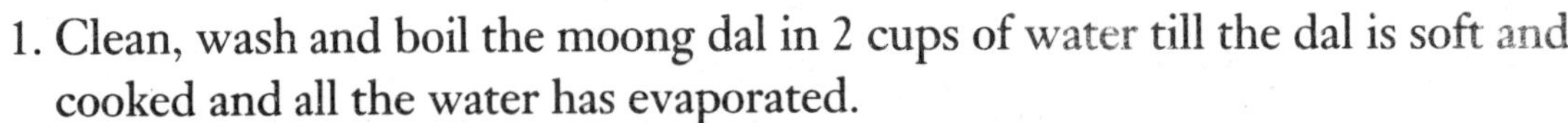

1. Clean, wash and boil the moong dal in 2 cups of water till the dal is soft and cooked and all the water has evaporated.
2. Combine the cooked dal with the rest of the ingredients and mix well.
3. Divide the mixture into 12 equal portions.
4. Using a thick seekh (metal skewer), press each portion of the dal mixture on it using your fingers to make a 100 mm. (4") long kebab.
5. Brush each kebab very lightly with oil.

6. Cook the kebabs over a grill or over a charcoal barbeque till the kebabs are evenly browned (approx. 3 to 4 minutes).
7. Cut into pieces and serve hot, with mint and coriander chutney.

Nutritive values per kebab :

AMT	ENERGY	PROTEIN	CHO	FAT	VIT.A	VIT.C	CALCIUM	IRON	F.ACID	FIBRE
gm	kcal	gm	gm	gm	mcg	mg	mg	mg	mcg	gm
14	31	1.7	4.9	0.5	42.2	1.6	7.5	0.3	9.3	0.1

Sprouts Chaat

Preparation time :
10 minutes.
Cooking time :
25 minutes.
Serves 3.

We usually associate chaat with unhealthy fried foods or ones that have been cooked using loads of oil. Sprouts chaat is a healthy variation which has all the flavour and none of the calories we relate chaat with.
Sprouts provide plenty of protein, vitamin C and iron to your diet and the protein content is further enhanced by the addition of steamed gram flour dumplings.

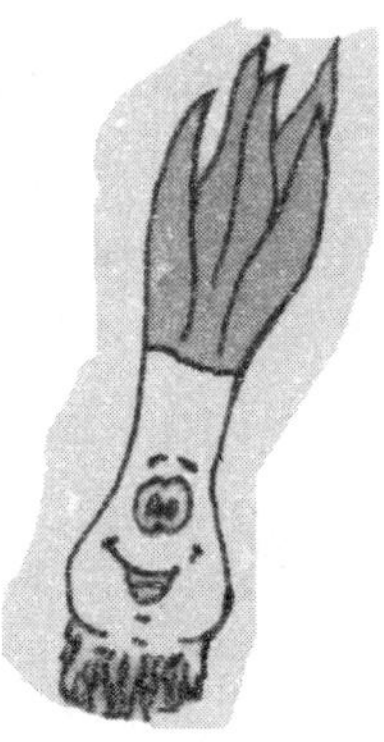

1½ cups moong sprouts
¾ cup onions, finely chopped
½ teaspoon cumin seeds (jeera)
½ teaspoon fennel seeds (saunf)
a pinch asafoetida (hing)
¼ teaspoon turmeric powder (haldi)
1 green chilli, finely chopped
1 teaspoon chaat masala
1 teaspoon sugar
2 teaspoons lemon juice
1 teaspoon oil
salt to taste

For the dumplings

½ cup Bengal gram flour (besan)
1 teaspoon chilli powder
½ teaspoon fennel seeds (saunf)
⅛ teaspoon ajwain (carom seeds)
2 to 3 tablespoons low fat curds, page 143
a pinch soda bi-carb
salt to taste

For the garnish

1 tablespoon chopped coriander

For the dumplings

1. Combine all the ingredients and knead into a smooth dough.
2. Divide the dough into 4 equal portions.
3. Shape each portion to make a thin roll approximately 6 mm. (¼") in diameter.
4. Steam the rolls for 8 to 10 minutes.
5. Cool completely and cut the rolls into very small pieces. Keep aside.

How to proceed

1. Heat the oil in a non-stick pan and add the cumin seeds, fennel seeds and asafoetida.
2. When the seeds crackle, add the onions, turmeric powder and green chilli and sauté for 3 to 4 minutes.
3. Add the moong sprouts, salt and ¼ cup of water and cook for 4 to 5 minutes.
4. Add the prepared dumplings, chaat masala, sugar and lemon juice and mix well.

   Serve hot, garnished with the coriander.

Nutritive values per serving :

AMT	ENERGY	PROTEIN	CHO	FAT	VIT.A	VIT.C	CALCIUM	IRON	F.ACID	FIBRE
gm	kcal	gm	gm	gm	mcg	mg	mg	mg	mcg	gm
86	188	10.3	30.2	2.9	127.2	7.8	80.2	2.2	22.1	1.6

Cabbage Jowar Muthias

Preparation time :
10 minutes.

Cooking time :
15 minutes.

Serves 4.

Muthias are an all time favourite snack for Gujaratis, but for some people they may be very new. These are steamed dumplings that can be made with 2 or 3 kinds of flour combinations and can be flavoured with different vegetables like methi, mooli (radish), bottle gourd (doodhi / lauki) etc.
This version uses cabbage and jowar flour to provide you with plenty of fibre and flavour.
You can try eating these to lower down your caloric intake but do remember to limit the oil used for the tempering. These muthias make a great snack, accompanied by a fruit or a fruit juice.

For the muthias

1 cup grated cabbage
1 cup jowar flour (white millet flour)
5 tablespoons low fat curds, page 143
1 tablespoon chopped coriander
juice of ½ lemon
1 teaspoon ginger-green chilli paste
2 large cloves garlic, grated
½ teaspoon turmeric powder (haldi)
a pinch soda bi-carb
1 tablespoon sugar
salt to taste

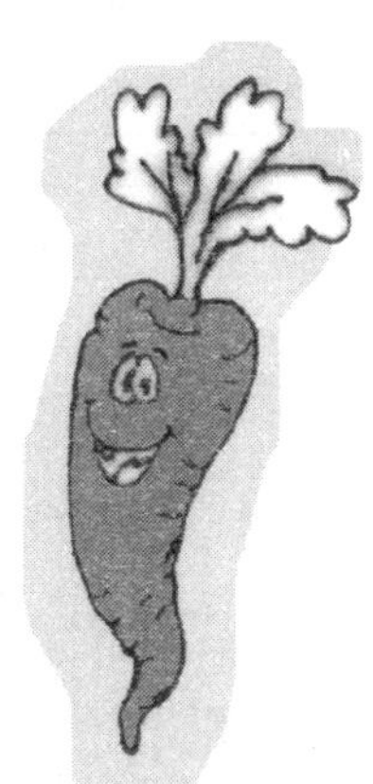

For the tempering

1 teaspoon cumin seeds (jeera)
¼ teaspoon asafoetida (hing)
3 to 4 curry leaves
1 teaspoon oil

For the garnish

2 tablespoons chopped coriander

Other ingredients

oil for greasing

For the muthias

1. Combine all the ingredients in a bowl and knead to make a soft dough using enough water.
2. Divide the dough into a 3 equal parts and shape each portion into a cylindrical roll of approx. 125 mm. (5") in length.
3. Place the rolls on a greased steaming dish and steam for 10 to 12 minutes till firm.
4. Remove, cool and cut into 25 mm (1") thick slices.

How to proceed

1. Heat the oil in a non-stick pan and add the cumin seeds. When they crackle, add the asafoetida and curry leaves.
2. Add the sliced muthias and sauté over a slow flame till they are lightly browned.

Serve hot, garnished with the coriander.

Nutritive values per serving :

AMT	ENERGY	PROTEIN	CHO	FAT	VIT.A	VIT.C	CALCIUM	IRON	F.ACID	FIBRE
gm	kcal	gm	gm	gm	mcg	mg	mg	mg	mcg	gm
58	127	3.7	24.0	1.8	203.0	30.0	46.6	1.2	9.6	0.7

Tandoori Mushrooms

Picture on page 58

Preparation time :
10 minutes.
Cooking time :
10 minutes.
Serves 4.

Mushrooms are low in calories and are a valuable source of protein. The aroma of these velvety textured mushrooms is simply irresistible. Serve these tandoori mushrooms as starters to a main meal.
If you're not very fond of mushrooms, try using low fat paneer, page 144, or baby corn pieces instead.

300 grams mushrooms, cut into half
½ cup low fat milk, page 142
½ teaspoon cornflour
½ teaspoon kasuri methi (dried fenugreek leaves)
1 teaspoon oil
salt to taste

To be ground into a paste

4 whole red chillies
4 large cloves garlic
25 mm. (1") piece ginger
2 teaspoons coriander-cumin seed (dhania-jeera) powder

1. Wash the mushrooms thoroughly. Drain and keep aside.
2. Dissolve the cornflour in the milk and keep aside.
3. Heat the oil in a non-stick pan, add the prepared chilli-garlic paste and kasuri methi and sauté for 1 minute.
4. Add the mushrooms, cornflour-milk mixture and salt and sauté for 4 to 5 minutes till the mixture coats the mushrooms.
   Serve hot.

Nutritive values per serving :

AMT	ENERGY	PROTEIN	CHO	FAT	VIT.A	VIT.C	CALCIUM	IRON	F.ACID	FIBRE
gm	kcal	gm	gm	gm	mcg	mg	mg	mg	mcg	gm
79	40	2.5	4.9	1.6	11.5	2.8	38.1	1.0	15.9	1.0

Green Pea Pankis

Preparation time : 5 minutes.

Cooking time : 8 minutes.

Makes 14 pankis.

Panki is a popular Gujarati snack made of a rice flour batter that is cooked between 2 banana leaves. Green peas added to the panki batter make it look more appealing and enhance its fibre value. Serve these steaming hot pankis with the spicy Mint and Coriander Chutney, page 147.

⅓ cup rice flour (chawal ka atta)
1 tablespoon urad dal (split black lentils) flour
1 teaspoon low fat curds, page 143
1 to 2 green chillies, finely chopped
¼ cup boiled green peas, coarsely ground
2 tablespoons chopped coriander
½ teaspoon cumin seeds (jeera), crushed
salt to taste

Other ingredients

3 banana leaves
1 teaspoon oil for greasing

For serving

mint and coriander chutney, page 147

1. In a bowl, combine the rice flour, urad dal flour, curds, green chillies, green peas, coriander, cumin seeds, salt and approx. ½ cup of water. Mix well to make a thin batter.
2. Cut the banana leaves into circles using a 75 mm. (3") diameter cookie cutter.
3. Apply a little oil on each banana leaf.
4. Heat a tava (griddle) and arrange half of the banana leaf circles on the tava.
5. Spread 2 teaspoons of the batter on each leaf and sandwich with another greased banana leaf on top.

6. Cook the pankis on both sides till light brown spots appear on the banana leaves and the pancake in between peels off the banana leaf easily.
Serve hot, with mint and coriander chutney.

Handy Tip *If you do not have a cookie cutter for cutting the banana leaves into circles, cut them in squares and proceed as per the recipe.*

Variation : *You can use grated paneer, cabbage, carrots instead of green peas for the above recipe.*

Nutritive values per panki :

AMT	ENERGY	PROTEIN	CHO	FAT	VIT.A	VIT.C	CALCIUM	IRON	F.ACID	FIBRE
gm	kcal	gm	gm	gm	mcg	mg	mg	mg	mcg	gm
7	19	0.6	3.2	0.4	35.3	0.8	3.2	0.1	1.6	0.1

Lapsi Methi Muthias

Preparation time :
10 minutes.

Cooking time :
30 minutes.

Serves *4.*

Another fibre rich snack that abounds in iron and vitamin A. These delectable muthias are sure to keep you 'full' for a long time.
These are slightly more crumbly than regular muthias because of the broken wheat, but I guarantee you will love them.

For the muthias

½ cup broken wheat (dalia)
½ cup fenugreek (methi) leaves, finely chopped
¼ cup bajra flour (black millet flour)
2 large cloves garlic, grated
1 teaspoon ginger-green chilli paste
1 teaspoon sugar
a pinch soda bi-carb

1/8 teaspoon turmeric powder (haldi)
2 tablespoons low fat curds, page 143
salt to taste

For the tempering

1 teaspoon oil
1/2 teaspoon mustard seeds (rai)
a pinch asafoetida (hing)

For the garnish

1 tablespoon chopped coriander

For the muthias

1. Clean and wash the broken wheat.
2. Blanch the broken wheat in boiling water for 8 to 10 minutes. Drain completely and keep aside.
3. Combine all the ingredients in a bowl and mix well.
4. Divide the muthia mixture into 8 equal portions. Shape each portion into a cylindrical roll 100 mm. (4") in length and 12 mm. (½") in diameter.
5. Steam the rolls for 12 to 15 minutes or till a knife inserted in a roll comes out clean.
6. Cool and slice the muthias into 12 mm. (½") long pieces and keep aside.

How to proceed

1. Heat the oil in a non-stick pan, add the mustard seeds and asafoetida.
2. When the seeds crackle, add the prepared muthias and sauté for 3 to 4 minutes till they are light brown in colour.

   Serve hot, garnished with the coriander.

Nutritive values per serving :

AMT	ENERGY	PROTEIN	CHO	FAT	VIT.A	VIT.C	CALCIUM	IRON	F.ACID	FIBRE
gm	kcal	gm	gm	gm	mcg	mg	mg	mg	mcg	gm
32	108	2.7	20.2	1.9	153.0	2.9	34.8	1.5	2.7	0.4

Swadisht Vegetable Rolls

Picture on page 58

Preparation time :
10 minutes.
Cooking time :
20 minutes.
Makes 10 rolls.

These delectable low fat vegetable rolls are perfect for an afternoon snack. Carrots are a valuable source of vitamin A and are packed with a variety of ingredients to make these delicious rolls which I am sure most of us will enjoy ! Relish them with Mint and Coriander Chutney, page 147, for a satiating guilt-free snack.

1 cup carrots, grated
2 medium raw bananas
¼ teaspoon mustard seeds (rai)
¼ teaspoon urad dal (split black lentils)
½ cup onions, finely chopped
1 teaspoon ginger-green chilli paste
2 tablespoons chopped coriander
½ teaspoon chilli powder
½ teaspoon chaat masala
½ teaspoon lemon juice
½ teaspoon oil
salt to taste

Other ingredients

½ teaspoon oil for cooking

For serving

mint and coriander chutney, page 147

1. Pressure cook the whole raw bananas till they are soft and cooked.
2. Peel the bananas and grate them.
3. Heat the oil in a non-stick pan, add the mustard seeds and urad dal.
4. When the seeds crackle, add the onions, carrots, grated bananas and ginger-green chilli paste and sauté for 3 to 4 minutes. Remove from the fire.

5. Add the coriander, chilli powder, chaat masala, lemon juice and salt and mix well.
6. Divide the mixture into 10 equal portions and shape into cylindrical rolls.
7. Cook the rolls on a non-stick pan, using the oil till they are golden brown. Serve hot, with mint and coriander chutney.

Nutritive values per roll :

AMT	ENERGY	PROTEIN	CHO	FAT	VIT.A	VIT.C	CALCIUM	IRON	F.ACID	FIBRE
gm	kcal	gm	gm	gm	mcg	mg	mg	mg	mcg	gm
29	20	0.4	3.4	0.6	215.8	4.7	12.9	0.9	3.7	0.2

Paneer Tikka Kathi Rolls

Picture on cover

Preparation time : 15 minutes.

Cooking time : 20 minutes.

Makes 9 rolls.

These rolls are a healthy version of frankies and make a complete meal by themselves. The chapatis have been made with whole wheat flour which is a good source of iron and fibre as compared to the usual plain flour (maida) rotis.
The paneer and vegetable filling enriches these rolls with essential vitamins and minerals and the calcium packed marinade adds an extra 'zing' to this recipe.

For the paneer tikka filling

1 cup low fat paneer, page 144, cubed
½ cup tomatoes, deseeded and diced
½ cup capsicum, diced
1 teaspoon oil

To be mixed into a marinade

¼ cup low fat curds, page 143, beaten
1 teaspoon chilli powder
¼ teaspoon turmeric powder (haldi)
½ teaspoon ginger paste
¼ teaspoon garlic paste
¼ teaspoon Bengal gram flour (besan)
½ teaspoon chaat masala
½ teaspoon kasuri methi (dried fenugreek leaves)
½ teaspoon garam masala
salt to taste

For the chapatis

1 cup whole wheat flour (gehun ka atta)
¾ cup low fat milk, page 142
salt to taste

For the paneer tikka filling

1. Add the paneer and tomatoes to the prepared marinade and toss lightly.
2. Leave aside for 10 minutes.
3. Heat the oil in a non-stick pan, add the capsicum and sauté for 2 minutes.
4. Add the paneer mixture and sauté over a high flame for 4 to 5 minutes, stirring occasionally.

For the chapatis

1. Combine all the ingredients and knead into a soft dough.
2. Divide the dough into 9 equal portions.
3. Roll out each portion into a thin chapati.
4. Cook each chapati lightly on a tava (griddle) on both sides. Keep aside.

How to proceed

1. Divide the paneer tikka filling into 9 equal portions.
2. Spread one portion of the filling in the centre of each chapati and roll up tightly.
3. When you want to serve, cook the rolls on a hot tava (griddle).
4. Cut into 50 mm. (2") long pieces and serve hot.

Handy Tip *Wrap each roll in a lettuce leaf as I have done in the picture on the cover. You can also use a scooped carrot slice to hold the roll together. It is easy and looks great too.*

Nutritive values per roll :

AMT	ENERGY	PROTEIN	CHO	FAT	VIT.A	VIT.C	CALCIUM	IRON	F.ACID	FIBRE
gm	kcal	gm	gm	gm	mcg	mg	mg	mg	mcg	gm
37	81	5.0	13.5	0.8	67.8	12.1	132.4	0.8	6.9	0.4

Any Time Munchies

Masala Khakhras

Picture on page 75

Preparation time :
10 minutes.

Cooking time :
15 minutes.

Makes *4 khakhras.*

Spicy cumin and whole wheat khakhras. I usually make a large batch of these and store them in an air-tight container for those hungry times. They stay well for several days and make an ideal low calorie snack for you and your family. With a little imagination and a wee bit of effort, you can spice them differently or even experiment with different kinds of flours like jowar, bajra to make delicious low calorie munchies.

½ cup whole wheat flour (gehun ka atta)
1 teaspoon Bengal gram flour (besan)
¼ teaspoon cumin seeds (jeera)
⅛ teaspoon chilli powder
a pinch turmeric powder (haldi)
a pinch asafoetida (hing)
4 tablespoons low fat milk, page 142
1 teaspoon oil
salt to taste

1. Mix all the ingredients and knead into a soft dough.
2. Divide the dough into 4 equal portions and roll out each portion into a very thin round of 150 mm. (6") diameter using a little flour.
3. Cook each khakhra on a hot tava (griddle) on both sides until brown spots appear on the surface.

1. Melon Tango, *page 38*
2. Muesli, *page 24*

4. With the help of a folded muslin cloth, press the khakhra from all the sides and cook over a slow flame till it is crisp.
   Store in an air-tight container.

Nutritive values per khakhra :

AMT	ENERGY	PROTEIN	CHO	FAT	VIT.A	VIT.C	CALCIUM	IRON	F.ACID	FIBRE
gm	kcal	gm	gm	gm	mcg	mg	mg	mg	mcg	gm
17	65	2.4	10.6	1.5	16.1	0.1	27.5	0.7	5.9	0.3

Baked Methi Muthias

Preparation time :
10 minutes.
Baking time :
7 to 8 minutes.
Baking temperature :
200°C (400°F).
Makes 8 muthias.

Traditionally muthias are either steamed or fried, but I have baked them here with just a teaspoon of oil and ended up with splendid results. A tasty way to get a light baked snack on the table in a jiffy. Fenugreek (methi) leaves enrich this recipe with vitamin A, iron and calcium. These methi muthias are sure to gather praise from all those who taste this wonderful and attractive creation.
These can also be added to a tomato gravy to make a delightful vegetable dish served along with phulkas.

1 cup fenugreek (methi) leaves, chopped
1/3 cup whole wheat flour (gehun ka atta)
1/3 cup Bengal gram flour (besan)

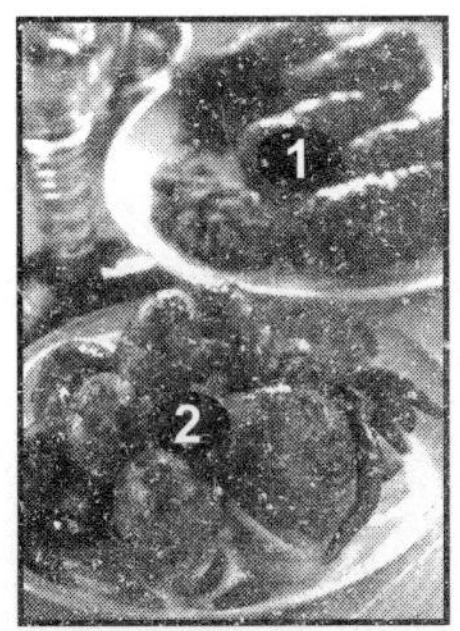

1. Swadisht Vegetable Rolls, *page 51*
2. Tandoori Mushrooms, *page 47*

½ teaspoon ginger-green chili paste
1 teaspoon sugar
1 teaspoon lemon juice
¼ teaspoon turmeric powder (haldi)
¼ teaspoon garam masala
1 teaspoon oil
salt to taste

Other ingredients

oil for greasing

1. Mix all the ingredients in a bowl and knead into a soft dough using a little water.
2. Divide the dough into 8 equal portions, shape into even sized rounds and flatten them by placing between your palms.
3. Place on a greased baking tray and bake in a pre-heated oven at 200°C (400°F) for 7 to 8 minutes.

Serve hot.

Nutritive values per muthia :

AMT	ENERGY	PROTEIN	CHO	FAT	VIT.A	VIT.C	CALCIUM	IRON	F.ACID	FIBRE
gm	kcal	gm	gm	gm	mcg	mg	mg	mg	mcg	gm
14	38	1.4	6.1	0.9	93.2	2.3	18.8	0.5	6.6	0.2

Baked Chaklis

Picture on page 75

Preparation time :
10 minutes.
Baking time :
15 minutes.

Baking temperature :
160°C (320°F).

Makes 12 chaklis.

This simple and delicious recipe is a real treat for weight watchers. Chaklis, the popular Indian snack, is usually deep fried and contains loads of calories. Here's how to make them with 1 teaspoon of oil to near perfection by baking them in an oven.
Munch them at anytime of the day when hunger strikes.

½ cup rice flour (chawal ka atta)
1 teaspoon oil
1 tablespoon low fat curds, page 143
a pinch asafoetida (hing)
salt to taste

Other ingredients

oil for greasing

1. Combine the rice flour, oil, asafoetida and salt in a bowl and mix well.
2. Add the curds and a little water and knead into a soft dough.
3. Put the mixture into a chakli press and press out round whirls of the dough onto a greased baking tray, working closely from the centre to the outside to the whirl (approximately 50 mm. (2") diameter). You will get about 12 chaklis.
4. Bake these chaklis in a pre-heated oven at 160°C (320°F) for 10 to 15 minutes. When one side of the chakli turns golden brown in colour, gently flip over the chakli using a flat spoon and bake till they are light brown in colour.
Store in an air-tight container.

Nutritive values per chakli :

AMT	ENERGY	PROTEIN	CHO	FAT	VIT.A	VIT.C	CALCIUM	IRON	F.ACID	FIBRE
gm	kcal	gm	gm	gm	mcg	mg	mg	mg	mcg	gm
6	21	0.4	4.0	0.4	3.8	0.0	2.2	0.0	0.4	0.0

Low Cal Chivda

Preparation time :
5 minutes.
Cooking time :
8 minutes.
Serves 4.

A delectable snack made using flaked rice seasoned with the right blend of spices.
Use a thin variety of poha commonly known as "nylon poha", to make a crispier snack. This chivda can be stored in an air-tight container for several days.
This guilt-free chivda is a good option for a mid-morning or an evening snack.

1 cup poha (beaten rice flakes)
1 teaspoon raw peanuts (optional)
¼ teaspoon mustard seeds (rai)
2 green chillies, slit lengthwise
4 to 5 curry leaves
1 tablespoon roasted chana dal (daria)
a pinch asafoetida (hing)
a pinch turmeric powder (haldi)
1 teaspoon powdered sugar
1 teaspoon oil
salt to taste

1. Roast the poha and peanuts in a non-stick pan, stirring occasionally till the poha is crisp (approx. 3 to 4 minutes).
2. Heat the oil in a non-stick pan, add the mustard seeds, green chillies, curry leaves and roasted chana dal and stir.
3. When the seeds crackle, add the asafoetida and turmeric powder and mix well.
4. Add the roasted poha and peanuts, sugar and salt and mix well.
   Cool and store in an air-tight container.

Nutritive values per serving :

AMT	ENERGY	PROTEIN	CHO	FAT	VIT.A	VIT.C	CALCIUM	IRON	F.ACID	FIBRE
gm	kcal	gm	gm	gm	mcg	mg	mg	mg	mcg	gm
22	83	1.8	15.2	1.7	16.4	0.0	5.2	3.2	5.9	0.2

Palak Methi Puris

Preparation time :
10 minutes.

Baking time :
15 minutes.

Baking temperature :
180°C (360°F).

Makes 35 puris.

These low calorie puris are a great way of disguising dark green leafy vegetables. Palak and methi are both very good sources of vitamin A which is necessary for maintaining a healthy vision and a glowing complexion. Though baked only with 1 teaspoon of oil and not deep fried, these puris are really crisp.
They make an excellent tea-time snack and are sure to keep you going until dinner.

½ cup spinach (palak), chopped
¼ cup fenugreek (methi) leaves, chopped
¼ cup jowar flour (white millet flour)
¼ cup bajra flour (black millet flour)
2 tablespoons whole wheat flour (gehun ka atta)
1 teaspoon ginger-green chilli paste
1 teaspoon oil
salt to taste

1. Combine the spinach and fenugreek, add salt and allow to rest for 10 minutes till the liquid is released. Use this liquid to bind the puri dough. Add all the other ingredients and knead into a soft dough, using a little water if required.
2. Divide the dough into 35 equal portions.
3. Roll out each portion into a circle of 37 mm. (1½") diameter.
4. Prick the rolled out puris with a fork at regular intervals.

5. Bake in a pre-heated oven at 180°C (360°F) for 10 to 12 minutes or till the puris are golden brown.
Store in an air-tight container.

Nutritive values per puri :

AMT	ENERGY	PROTEIN	CHO	FAT	VIT.A	VIT.C	CALCIUM	IRON	F.ACID	FIBRE
gm	kcal	gm	gm	gm	mcg	mg	mg	mg	mcg	gm
3	8	0.2	1.4	0.2	61.5	0.4	2.2	0.1	1.8	0.0

Tongue Tickling Subjis

Methi Mutter Pasanda

Preparation time :
15 minutes.
Cooking time :
30 minutes.
Serves 4.

This recipe is an all time favourite. Puréed cauliflower perked with onion and spices imparts a creamy texture to this subji and eliminates the use of high calorie ingredients such as cream and cashewnuts.
Methi has plenty of iron and vitamin A while fresh green peas provide fibre which adds bulk and satiates your appetite. This recipe is a perfect accompaniment for Nutritious Garlic Naans, page 113.

1 cup green peas, boiled
1 cup fenugreek (methi) leaves, finely chopped
¼ teaspoon cumin seeds (jeera)
½ teaspoon kasuri methi (dried fenugreek leaves)
¼ cup low fat milk, page 142
¼ cup low fat curds, page 143
½ teaspoon Bengal gram flour (besan)
¼ teaspoon garam masala
1 teaspoon oil
salt to taste

For the paste

1¼ cups sliced onions
¼ cup cauliflower, finely chopped
1 to 2 green chillies, chopped
2 large cloves garlic, chopped
12 mm. (½") piece ginger, sliced
1 stick cinnamon (dalchini)
1 clove (laung)
1 cup low fat milk, page 142

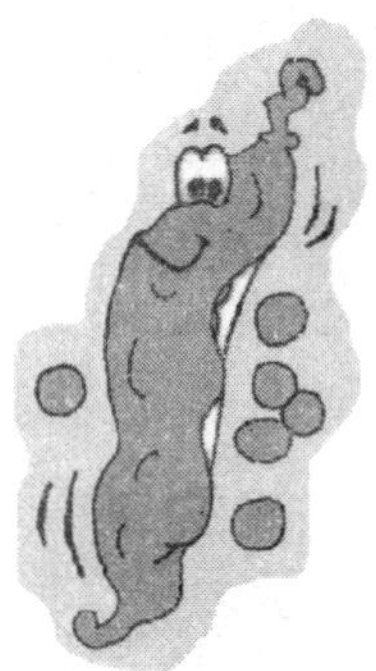

For the paste

1. Combine all the ingredients in a pan and simmer for 8 to 10 minutes till the onions are soft and nearly all the liquid has evaporated.
2. Purée the mixture to a smooth paste in a blender. Keep aside.

How to proceed

1. Combine the milk, curds and gram flour. Mix well and keep aside.
2. Sprinkle salt over the fenugreek leaves and leave aside for 10 minutes. Wash the fenugreek leaves well. Squeeze out all the water.
3. Heat the oil in a non-stick pan and add the cumin seeds.
4. When the seeds crackle, add the fenugreek leaves and kasuri methi and sauté for 3 to 4 minutes.
5. Add the prepared paste, curd-gram flour mixture, garam masala and salt with ½ cup of water and bring the mixture to a boil.
6. Add the green peas and simmer for 1 to 2 minutes.
   Serve hot.

Nutritive values per serving :

AMT	ENERGY	PROTEIN	CHO	FAT	VIT.A	VIT.C	CALCIUM	IRON	F.ACID	FIBRE
gm	kcal	gm	gm	gm	mcg	mg	mg	mg	mcg	gm
74	86	6.1	12.2	1.4	205.8	11.8	147.8	0.9	4.6	1.6

Paneer Palak Koftas in Makhani Gravy

Preparation time :
15 minutes.

Cooking time :
25 minutes.

Serves 4.

This dish has been specially prepared for calorie conscious North Indian food fans. Take my word for it — these steamed koftas in a nourishing makhani gravy are really "finger licking". Serve it with Saatdhan Pararthas, page 112, to make a sumptuous meal.

For the paneer palak koftas

½ cup spinach (palak), blanched, drained and chopped
½ cup low fat paneer, page 144, grated
3 teaspoons rice flour (chawal ka atta)
½ green chilli, finely chopped
salt to taste

For the makhani gravy

3 cups tomatoes, chopped
½ cup onion, chopped
2 large cloves garlic, chopped
12 mm. (½") piece ginger, chopped
2 cloves (laung)
1 stick cinnamon (dalchini)
¼ cup red pumpkin (kaddu), chopped
½ teaspoon cumin seeds (jeera)
¼ teaspoon kasuri methi (dried fenugreek leaves)
1 teaspoon chilli powder
½ cup low fat milk, page 142
½ teaspoon cornflour
½ teaspoon sugar
1 teaspoon oil
salt to taste

For the paneer palak koftas

1. Combine all the ingredients in a bowl and mix well.
2. Divide the mixture into 12 equal portions. Shape each portion into an even sized round.
3. Steam the koftas for 4 to 5 minutes. Keep aside.

For the makhani gravy

1. Combine the tomatoes, onion, garlic, ginger, cloves, cinnamon and red pumpkin with 1 cup of water and cook over a slow flame till the vegetables are soft. Allow to cool completely. Remove the cinnamon & cloves and discard.
2. Blend the tomato mixture to a smooth purée.
3. Heat the oil in a non-stick pan and add the cumin seeds.
4. When the seeds crackle, add the kasuri methi and chilli powder and sauté for a few seconds.
5. Add the puréed vegetable mixture, sugar and salt and bring to a boil.
6. Dissolve the cornflour in the milk and add it to the prepared gravy. Simmer for a few minutes.

How to proceed

Add the paneer palak koftas to the hot makhani gravy and mix well.
Serve hot.

Handy Tips

1. *Adjust the consistency of the gravy by adding water if necessary before serving.*
2. *2½ cups chopped spinach gives you approx. ½ cup of blanched and chopped spinach.*
3. *Squeeze out all the water from the blanched spinach to make koftas.*

Nutritive values per serving :

AMT	ENERGY	PROTEIN	CHO	FAT	VIT.A	VIT.C	CALCIUM	IRON	F.ACID	FIBRE
gm	kcal	gm	gm	gm	mcg	mg	mg	mg	mcg	gm
199	103	6.2	15.3	1.8	2797.7	46.0	233.0	1.5	89.6	1.4

Palak Baby Corn Subji

This is a low cal version of palak paneer in which I have used baby corn instead. Baby corn apart form being low in calories and fat as compared to other vegetables also imparts a crispy texture to the subji.

Preparation time :
10 minutes.

Cooking time :
15 minutes.

Serves *4.*

1 bunch spinach (palak)
½ cup baby corn, blanched and sliced
½ teaspoon cumin seeds (jeera)
¼ teaspoon asafoetida (hing)
1 onion, finely chopped
¼ teaspoon kasuri methi (dried fenugreek leaves)
1 teaspoon coriander (dhania) powder
½ cup low fat milk, page 142
1 teaspoon oil
salt to taste

To be ground into a paste

3 cloves garlic
12 mm. (½") piece ginger
1 green chilli

1. Blanch the spinach in boiling water. Drain and purée to a smooth paste in a blender.
2. Heat the oil in a non-stick pan and add the cumin seeds and asafoetida.
3. When the seeds crackle, add the onion and prepared paste and sauté for 4 to 5 minutes till the onion turns golden brown in colour.
4. Add the kasuri methi and coriander powder and sauté for another minute.
5. Add the spinach purée, baby corn, milk and salt and bring to a boil.
   Serve hot.

Nutritive values per serving :

AMT	ENERGY	PROTEIN	CHO	FAT	VIT.A	VIT.C	CALCIUM	IRON	F.ACID	FIBRE
gm	kcal	gm	gm	gm	mcg	mg	mg	mg	mcg	gm
85	60	2.8	8.4	1.7	2652.4	16.4	79.3	0.9	59.3	0.7

Bharva Baingan

Preparation time :
10 minutes.
Cooking time :
20 minutes.
Serves 4.

Brinjals are delicate in flavour and absorb other flavours very well. In this recipe, I have used onions and potatoes to fill them along with a host of complimentary spices that enhance the taste of brinjals. The filling mixture of these brinjals abounds in vitamin C and iron.
Serve this vegetable with hot phulkas.

125 grams (approx. 6 nos) small brinjals (baingan)
½ teaspoon cumin seeds (jeera)
a pinch asafoetida (hing)
1 medium onion, finely chopped
1 small potato, grated
¼ teaspoon turmeric powder (haldi)
1 teaspoon chilli powder
1 teaspoon Bengal gram flour (besan)
1 teaspoon tamarind (imli) pulp
1 teaspoon jaggery (gur), grated
¼ cup chopped coriander
½ tablespoon roasted chana dal (daria)
1 teaspoon oil
salt to taste

For the garnish

1 tablespoon chopped coriander

1. Heat the oil in a non-stick pan and add the cumin seeds and asafoetida.
2. When the seeds crackle, add the onion and sauté for 4 to 5 minutes till it turns golden brown in colour.
3. Add the potato, turmeric powder, chilli powder and gram flour and sauté for 2 to 3 minutes.
4. Add the tamarind pulp, jaggery, coriander, chana dal, salt and ½ cup of water and simmer till the mixture nearly dries up.
5. Remove the stems of the brinjals and make criss-cross slits on the brinjals, taking care not to separate the segments. Stuff the slits with the prepared masala mixture. About half the mixture will remain.
6. Combine the stuffed brinjals, the remaining masala mixture, salt and ¾ cup of water and pressure cook for 2 whistles.

Serve hot, garnished with the coriander.

Nutritive values per serving :

AMT	ENERGY	PROTEIN	CHO	FAT	VIT.A	VIT.C	CALCIUM	IRON	F.ACID	FIBRE
gm	kcal	gm	gm	gm	mcg	mg	mg	mg	mcg	gm
72	59	1.5	9.8	1.5	145.1	10.4	21.8	0.5	16.9	0.6

Dahi Bhindi ki Subji

Preparation time :
15 minutes.
Cooking time :
15 minutes.
Serves 4.

Here's a great way to enjoy a Rajasthani delicacy that is simply sumptuous and low in calories. Choose young and tender bhindis for this recipe that will cook quickly.
Above all, the rich and fascinating aroma is so tempting that you won't feel that you're eating low calorie food.

2 cups bhindi (ladies fingers), cut into 50 mm. (2") pieces
1 cup low fat curds, page 143
2 teaspoons coriander (dhania) powder

2 teaspoons chilli powder
½ teaspoon Bengal gram flour (besan)
1 teaspoon cumin seeds (jeera)
1 teaspoon mustard seeds (rai)
1 teaspoon fennel seeds (saunf)
⅛ teaspoon asafoetida (hing)
5 to 7 curry leaves
1 teaspoon oil
salt to taste

For the garnish

1 tablespoon chopped coriander

1. Steam the bhindi for 5 to 7 minutes till soft. Keep aside.
2. Combine the curds, coriander powder, chilli powder, gram flour and salt with 2 tablespoons of water and keep aside.
3. Heat the oil in a non-stick pan and add the cumin seeds, mustard seeds, fennel seeds, asafoetida and curry leaves.
4. When the seeds crackle, add the curd mixture and steamed bhindi and bring to a boil. Simmer for 3 to 4 minutes.

   Serve hot, garnished with the coriander.

Nutritive values per serving :

AMT	ENERGY	PROTEIN	CHO	FAT	VIT.A	VIT.C	CALCIUM	IRON	F.ACID	FIBRE
gm	kcal	gm	gm	gm	mcg	mg	mg	mg	mcg	gm
51	46	2.8	5.6	1.4	86.5	7.0	99.1	0.3	46.8	0.5

Healthy Oondhiya

Preparation time :
15 minutes.
Cooking time :
30 minutes.
Serves 6.

Startling though it may seem, here is a wonderful and healthy modification of the famous festive Gujarati dish which is ordinarily loaded with oil. I've changed this recipe and cut down on the oil along with the invisible fat which you get from coconut.
The methi muthias added to this recipe are baked to a wonderful rich golden brown colour that are very appealing and also cut down a lot of the calories you get in the fried version.
A good amount of iron and calcium is available from this hearty dish and this is sure to become your family favourite.

For the oondhiya

2 cups surti papadi (double beans)
1¼ cups kand (purple yam), peeled and cut into cubes
1 cup baby potatoes
1¼ cups sweet potatoes, peeled and cut into cubes
3 to 4 small brinjals
½ teaspoon carom seeds (ajwain)
a pinch soda bi-carb
salt to taste

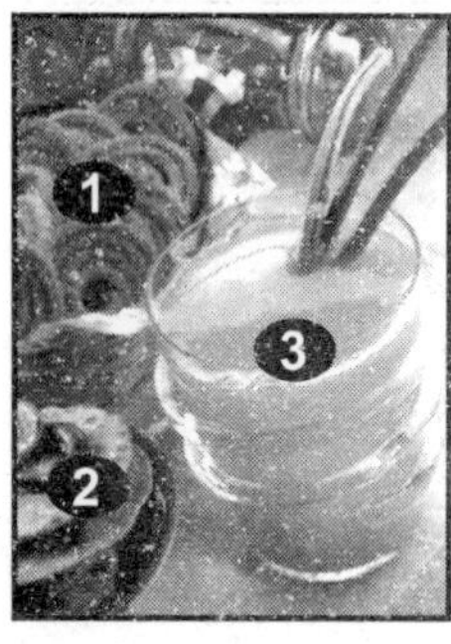

1. **Baked Chakiis,** *page 61*
2. **Masala Khakhras,** *page 56*
3. **Pineapple Celery Juice,** *page 39*

To be mixed into a masala

1 cup chopped coriander
½ cup poha (beaten rice flakes)
¼ cup green garlic, chopped
3 teaspoons coriander-cumin seed (dhania-jeera) powder
1 teaspoon ginger-green chilli paste
1 teaspoon chilli powder
1 teaspoon sugar
½ teaspoon carom seeds (ajwain)
¼ teaspoon turmeric powder (haldi)
¼ teaspoon asafoetida (hing)
1 ripe banana, mashed
salt to taste

Other ingredients

1 recipe baked methi muthias, page 59

For the garnish

1 tablespoon chopped coriander

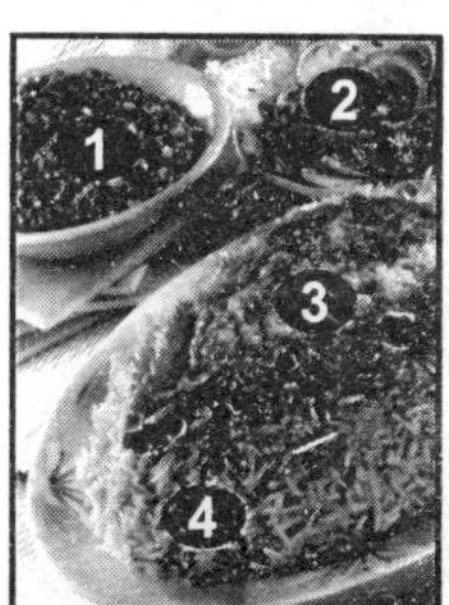

1. **Gajar Halwa,** *page 138*
2. **Spicy Kachumber,** *page 125*
3. **Dhan-saak Dal,** *page 95*
4. **Brown Rice,** *page 104*

For the oondhiya

1. String the surti papadi taking care not to separate the 2 sides.
2. Wash the papadi, add the carom seeds, soda bi-carb and salt and mix well.
3. Make criss-cross slits in the kand, baby potatoes, sweet potatoes and brinjals taking care not to separate the segments.
4. Fill half the masala mixture into the slits of kand, baby potatoes, sweet potatoes and brinjals. Keep aside the remaining masala mixture.
5. Combine the surti papadi, stuffed vegetables, remaining masala mixture with 3 cups of water and pressure cook for 2 whistles.

How to proceed

Transfer the cooked oondhiya, methi muthias into a large serving dish and toss lightly.

Serve hot, garnished with the coriander.

Nutritive values per serving :

AMT	ENERGY	PROTEIN	CHO	FAT	VIT.A	VIT.C	CALCIUM	IRON	F.ACID	FIBRE
gm	kcal	gm	gm	gm	mcg	mg	mg	mg	mcg	gm
169	197	5.2	40.6	1.6	498.4	24.2	74.1	2.7	24.0	1.7

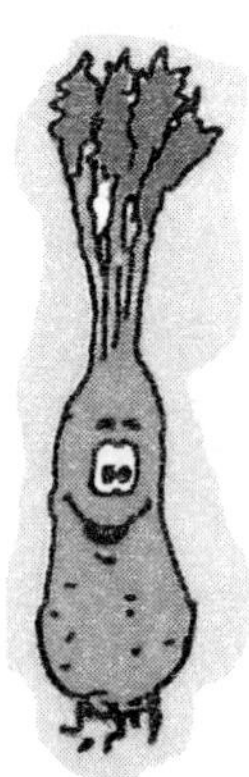

Dals and Kadhis

Dal Makhani

Preparation time :
15 minutes.

Cooking time :
20 to 25 minutes.

Serves 4.

Dal Makhani, a flavourful robust lentil preparation, is a celebrated delicacy from Punjab. Rajma and whole urad provide protein and calcium which are extremely important for maintenance of your body cells and healthy bones. Cooking the dal in tomato purée adds a little sharpness to this dish and also enriches it with folic acid and vitamin A.

Try this dal with Methi Makai ki Roti, page 110, to make a satisfying low fat meal.

½ cup whole urad (whole black lentils)
1 tablespoon rajma (kidney beans)
1 cup low fat milk, page 142
½ teaspoon cumin seeds (jeera)
½ cup onions, finely chopped
1 teaspoon ginger-garlic paste
1 teaspoon chilli powder
¼ teaspoon turmeric powder (haldi)
2 teaspoons coriander (dhania) powder
¾ cup fresh tomato pulp
1 teaspoon oil
salt to taste

For the garnish

2 tablespoons chopped coriander

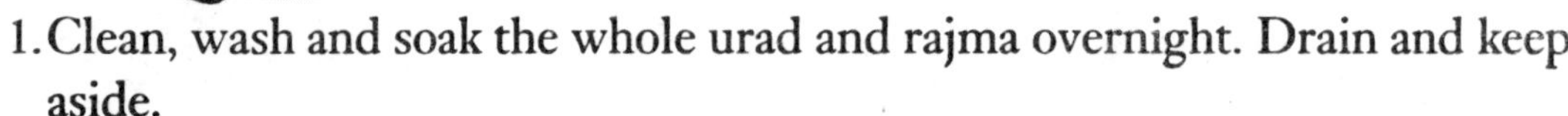

1. Clean, wash and soak the whole urad and rajma overnight. Drain and keep aside.
2. Combine the dals and salt with 2 cups of water and pressure cook till the dals are overcooked. Whisk well till the dal is almost mashed.
3. Add the milk and 1 cup of water and simmer for 10 minutes while stirring occasionally.

4. Heat the oil in a non-stick pan and add the cumin seeds. When the seeds crackle, add the onions and ginger-garlic paste and sauté till the onions turn golden brown.
5. Add the chilli powder, turmeric powder, coriander powder and tomato pulp with ¼ cup of water and sauté for 5 to 7 minutes.
6. Add this to the dal mixture and simmer for 10 to 12 minutes till the dal is thick and creamy.

Serve hot, garnished with the coriander.

Nutritive values per serving :

AMT	ENERGY	PROTEIN	CHO	FAT	VIT.A	VIT.C	CALCIUM	IRON	F.ACID	FIBRE
gm	kcal	gm	gm	gm	mcg	mg	mg	mg	mcg	gm
94	134	8.6	21.1	1.7	277.6	16.0	143.0	1.5	42.6	0.8

Vaal ki Usal

Picture on page 101

A popular, easy to make Maharashtrian dish. The combination of jaggery and kokum gives a sweet and tangy taste to the usal.

Vaal provides you the much needed protein, calcium and folic acid. Serve this usal with hot Palak aur Chawal ki Roti, page 111.

Preparation time : 10 minutes.

Cooking time : 25 minutes.

Serves 4.

2 cups sprouted vaal (field beans)
4 to 5 fresh kokums
1 teaspoon cumin seeds (jeera)
½ teaspoon asafoetida (hing)
5 to 6 curry leaves
1 teaspoon ginger, grated
1 cup onions, finely chopped
½ teaspoon turmeric powder (haldi)
3 teaspoons jaggery (gur), chopped
2 teaspoons chilli powder

4 tablespoons chopped coriander
1 teaspoon oil
salt to taste

1. Soak the kokums in 2 tablespoons of water and leave aside for 10 to 15 minutes. Purée the soaked kokums in a blender to get a smooth paste. Keep aside.
2. Heat the oil in a non-stick pan and add the cumin seeds. When they crackle, add the asafoetida, curry leaves and ginger and sauté for a few seconds.
3. Add the onions and sauté till they turn translucent.
4. Add the vaal and 1 cup of water. Cover and cook for 10 to 15 minutes.
5. Add the turmeric powder, kokum paste, jaggery, chilli powder, coriander and salt and cook for another 5 minutes.

   Serve hot.

Nutritive values per serving :

AMT	ENERGY	PROTEIN	CHO	FAT	VIT.A	VIT.C	CALCIUM	IRON	F.ACID	FIBRE
gm	kcal	gm	gm	gm	mcg	mg	mg	mg	mcg	gm
82	187	10.6	32.5	1.6	218.8	7.7	48.9	1.5	2.0	0.8

Kadhai Chole

Preparation time :
10 minutes.
Cooking time :
20 minutes.
Serves 4.

Chole, a traditional Punjabi dish, is usually made using a lot of fat. But this easy to make recipe is lower in calories and is just as tasty. The oil does not contribute much flavour, it is the spices that create this dish. Instead of bhature (deep fried puris), serve it with Nutritious Garlic Naans, page 113, which are healthy, nourishing and just as tasty.
It is important to soak the chick peas overnight to improve their digestibility and nutritive value by enhancing the protein, calcium and vitamin C levels.

1 cup chick peas (kabuli chana), soaked overnight
½ teaspoon cumin seeds (jeera)
⅓ cup onion, finely chopped
12 mm. (½") piece ginger, grated
2 cloves garlic, grated
½ cup tomatoes, chopped
2 teaspoons chole masala (chana masala)
1 teaspoon chilli powder
1 teaspoon amchur (dry mango) powder
¼ teaspoon turmeric powder (haldi)
2 teaspoons coriander (dhania) powder
1 teaspoon cumin seed (jeera) powder
1 teaspoon oil
salt to taste

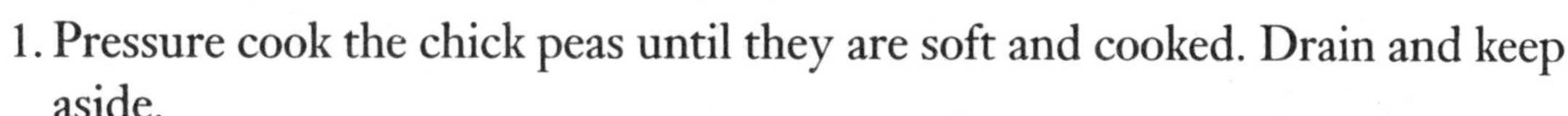

1. Pressure cook the chick peas until they are soft and cooked. Drain and keep aside.
2. Heat the oil in a non-stick pan, add the cumin seeds and fry. When the seeds crackle, add the onion, ginger and garlic and sauté till the onion turns golden brown. Add the tomatoes and sauté for 5 minutes.

3. Add the chole masala, chilli powder, amchur, turmeric powder, coriander powder, cumin seed powder and salt and sauté for another minute.
4. Add the chick peas and ½ cup of water and mix well. Simmer for 10 minutes.

Serve hot.

Handy Tip *Chole masala is a blend of spices, which is readily available at most grocery stores.*

Nutritive values per serving :

AMT	ENERGY	PROTEIN	CHO	FAT	VIT.A	VIT.C	CALCIUM	IRON	F.ACID	FIBRE
gm	kcal	gm	gm	gm	mcg	mg	mg	mg	mcg	gm
52	94	3.8	14.4	2.4	118.4	7.1	55.9	1.1	44.6	1.0

Radish Koftas in Kadhi

Picture on page 127

Preparation time : *15 minutes.*

Cooking time : *15 minutes.*

Serves 4.

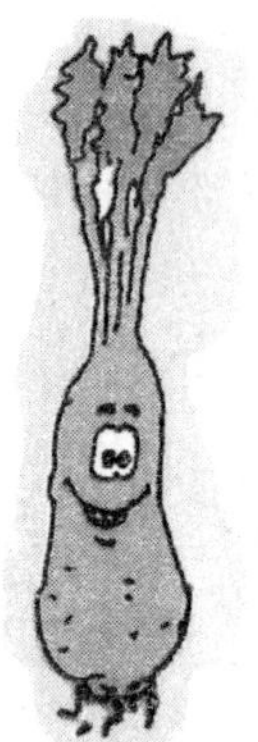

This simple combination of radish and low fat curds needs only steamed rice to complete your meal. You can adjust the consistency of the kadhi by varying the amount of water and besan. The radish koftas are steamed and not deep fried in the kadhi.

It is also a good way to add vegetables in your diet to provide vitamin A and iron. The curd and besan combination makes the kadhi a rich source of protein and calcium too.

For the radish koftas

¼ cup yellow moong dal (split yellow gram), soaked
¼ cup grated radish (mooli)
½ teaspoon ginger-green chilli paste
1 to 2 tablespoons Bengal gram flour (besan)
salt to taste

For the kadhi

1 cup low fat curds, page 143
2 tablespoons Bengal gram flour (besan)
1 teaspoon ginger-green chilli paste
a pinch turmeric powder (haldi)
1 teaspoon cumin seeds (jeera)
¼ teaspoon asafoetida (hing)
1 teaspoon oil
salt to taste

For the garnish

2 tablespoons chopped coriander

For the radish koftas

1. Drain out all the water from the dal and grind in a blender to a coarse paste, without using water.
2. Squeeze out all the liquid from the grated radish and add it to the ground moong dal. Use the radish liquid in the kadhi.
3. Add the ginger-green chilli paste, gram flour and salt and mix well. Keep aside the batter.

For the kadhi

1. Whisk the curds along with the gram flour till it is smooth and no lumps remain.
2. Add the ginger-green chilli paste and turmeric powder and mix well.
3. Heat the oil in a non-stick pan and add the cumin seeds. When they crackle, add the asafoetida.
4. Add the curds mixture and 2½ cups of water (inlcuding the liquid from the radish) and continue stirring till it comes to a boil.
5. Drop teaspoonfuls of the kofta mixture into the boiling kadhi and allow it to boil till the koftas are cooked (approx. 5 to 7 minutes).

Serve hot, garnished with the coriander.

Handy Tip *When you add the koftas into the kadhi, add one first and check to see that it does not crumble or disintegrate. If that happens, add some more gram flour to the kofta batter and check again.*

Nutritive values per serving :

AMT	ENERGY	PROTEIN	CHO	FAT	VIT.A	VIT.C	CALCIUM	IRON	F.ACID	FIBRE
gm	kcal	gm	gm	gm	mcg	mg	mg	mg	mcg	gm
30	86	5.6	12.2	1.7	127.6	3.3	84.1	0.8	22.2	0.2

Hariyali Dal

Preparation time :
15 minutes.
Cooking time :
25 minutes.
Serves 4.

Spinach and chana dal complement each other perfectly in this aromatic dish which is an excellent source of protein, iron, vitamin A and calcium. Try this dal with steamed rice or rotis. This is a good recipe for entertaining too!

½ cup split Bengal gram (chana dal)
1 bunch spinach (palak)
½ teaspoon cumin seeds (jeera)
⅛ teaspoon asafoetida (hing)
½ teaspoon kasuri methi (dried fenugreek leaves)
1 to 2 green chillies, finely chopped
¾ cup onions, finely chopped
1 teaspoon ginger paste
½ teaspoon garlic paste
½ teaspoon garam masala
1 teaspoon coriander (dhania) powder
¼ cup low fat milk, page 142
1 teaspoon oil
salt to taste

1. Clean and wash the chana dal and pressure cook it along with 1½ cups of water for 1 whistle. Drain and keep aside.
2. Boil plenty of water in a pan, add the spinach and cook for 2 to 3 minutes.
3. Drain the spinach and refresh it in ice-cold water. Drain again and purée it to a smooth paste in a blender. Keep aside.

4. Heat the oil in a non-stick pan and add the cumin seeds, asafoetida and kasuri methi.
5. When the seeds crackle, add the green chillies, onions, ginger paste and garlic paste and sauté till the onions turn golden brown in colour.
6. Add the garam masala, coriander powder and salt and cook for 1 minute.
7. Add the spinach purée, milk and ½ cup of water and cook for 3 to 4 minutes.
8. Add the cooked dal and simmer for 4 to 5 minutes.

Serve hot.

Nutritive values per serving :

AMT	ENERGY	PROTEIN	CHO	FAT	VIT.A	VIT.C	CALCIUM	IRON	F.ACID	FIBRE
gm	kcal	gm	gm	gm	mcg	mg	mg	mg	mcg	gm
95	117	6.0	17.0	2.8	2674.2	16.2	74.7	1.8	89.8	0.7

Tamatar ki Kadhi

Preparation time :
10 minutes.

Cooking time :
30 minutes.

Serves *4.*

Like many other dishes, kadhi differs from region to region. This Sindhi Kadhi is rather special as it is made using tomatoes. Tomatoes are very low in calories and provide plenty of vitamin A which is required for a glowing skin and healthy vision. I assure you that you and your family will relish this tangy kadhi with a touch of the sweetness provided by jaggery.

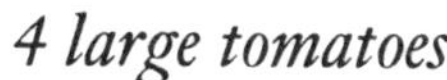

4 large tomatoes
½ teaspoon mustard seeds (rai)
½ teaspoon cumin seeds (jeera)
1 green chilli, chopped
5 to 6 curry leaves
2 sticks cinnamon (dalchini)
2 cloves (laung)
1 tablespoon Bengal gram flour (besan)

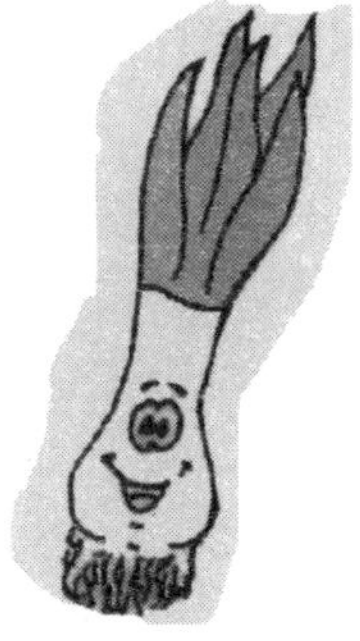

¼ teaspoon turmeric powder (haldi)
1 teaspoon chilli powder
a pinch asafoetida (hing)
2 teaspoons jaggery (gur), grated
1 teaspoon oil
salt to taste

For the garnish

1 tablespoon chopped coriander

1. Roughly chop the tomatoes and cook them with ½ cup of water for about 10 to 15 minutes.
2. Cool and liquidise the tomatoes in a food processor to a get a smooth purée. Strain the purée and keep aside.
3. Heat the oil in a non-stick pan and add the mustard seeds and cumin seeds.
4. When the seeds crackle, add the green chilli, curry leaves, cinnamon, cloves and gram flour and cook for 2 to 3 minutes.
5. Add the turmeric, chilli powder, asafoetida and puréed tomatoes with 2 cups of water and cook over a medium flame while stirring continuously.
6. When the kadhi comes to a boil, add the jaggery and salt and simmer for another 5 minutes. Remove from the fire.
7. Garnish with the coriander and serve hot with rice.

Handy Tip *If you find the kadhi to be too spicy, add 1 to 2 teaspoons of low fat milk to mellow it down.*

Nutritive values per serving :

AMT	ENERGY	PROTEIN	CHO	FAT	VIT.A	VIT.C	CALCIUM	IRON	F.ACID	FIBRE
gm	kcal	gm	gm	gm	mcg	mg	mg	mg	mcg	gm
85	46	1.2	6.9	1.5	339.5	22.1	42.3	0.7	26.4	0.7

Rasam

Preparation time :
10 minutes.
Cooking time :
20 minutes.
Serves 4.

A perfect recipe for you to enjoy the true flavours of home-made South Indian cooking. Serve this protein and vitamin packed rasam as an accompaniment to Nutritious Stuffed Idlis, page 25, or plain steamed rice and you're sure to love it.

2 tablespoons toovar (arhar) dal
1 small tomato, chopped
1½ teaspoons tamarind (imli), soaked in ¼ of cup water
1 recipe rasam powder, see below
⅛ teaspoon asafoetida (hing)
a pinch turmeric powder (haldi)
salt to taste

For the rasam powder

1 teaspoon coriander (dhania) seeds
3 whole red chillies, broken into pieces
5 to 6 peppercorns
1 teaspoon masoor dal (split red lentils)
½ teaspoon split Bengal gram (chana dal)
⅛ teaspoon cumin seeds (jeera)
4 to 6 curry leaves

For the tempering

1 teaspoon oil
¼ teaspoon mustard seeds (rai)
3 to 4 curry leaves

For the garnish

2 tablespoons chopped coriander

For the rasam powder

1. Roast all the ingredients in a pan for 3 to 4 minutes. Allow to cool completely.
2. Grind the mixture to a powder in a blender. Keep aside.

How to proceed

1. Combine the toovar dal with 1 cup of water and pressure cook for 2 to 3 whistles or until the dal is cooked.
2. Add the tomato and tamarind water to the cooked dal and simmer for 2 to 3 minutes.
3. Add the rasam powder, asafoetida, turmeric powder and salt with 3 cups of water and simmer for 8 to 10 minutes.
4. For the tempering, heat the oil in a pan and add the mustard seeds and curry leaves. When the seeds crackle, add the tempering to the prepared rasam and simmer for another 4 to 5 minutes.
   Serve hot, garnished with the coriander.

Nutritive values per serving :

AMT	ENERGY	PROTEIN	CHO	FAT	VIT.A	VIT.C	CALCIUM	IRON	F.ACID	FIBRE
gm	kcal	gm	gm	gm	mcg	mg	mg	mg	mcg	gm
32	47	2.3	6.2	1.5	197.0	7.3	18.7	0.5	15.0	0.3

Sprouted Kala Chana Ambti

Preparation time :
15 minutes.
Cooking time :
35 minutes.
Serves 3.

To my surprise, many of my friends were unaware that kala chana (black vatana) is available at most grocery shops. Therefore I've introduced this kala chana recipe for all its good protein qualities.
This pulse requires long and slow cooking similar to kidney beans (rajma) but sprouting helps to reduce its cooking time and adds on to its vitamin and mineral content.

1 cup sprouted kala chana (black vatana)
1 tablespoon tamarind (imli)
¼ teaspoon mustard seeds (rai)
¼ teaspoon asafoetida (hing)
2 whole red chillies, broken into pieces
3 cloves garlic, chopped
1 green chilli, chopped
½ teaspoon turmeric powder (haldi)
1 teaspoon grated jaggery (gur)
¼ teaspoon ajwain (carom seeds), crushed
1 teaspoon oil
salt to taste

1. Wash the chana and pressure cook it for 3 to 4 whistles. Drain and keep aside.
2. Mix the tamarind with ½ cup of water and leave aside for 10 minutes. Squeeze out tamarind water and keep aside.
3. Heat the oil in a non-stick pan, add the mustard seeds, asafoetida and red chillies.
4. When the seeds crackle, add the garlic, green chilli and the tamarind water and mix well.
5. Add the turmeric, jaggery, cooked chana, ajwain and salt and boil over a high flame for 5 to 7 minutes.

   Serve hot.

Nutritive values per serving :

AMT	ENERGY	PROTEIN	CHO	FAT	VIT.A	VIT.C	CALCIUM	IRON	F.ACID	FIBRE
gm	kcal	gm	gm	gm	mcg	mg	mg	mg	mcg	gm
24	97	3.5	14.5	2.8	54.1	0.6	43.3	1.0	38.4	0.8

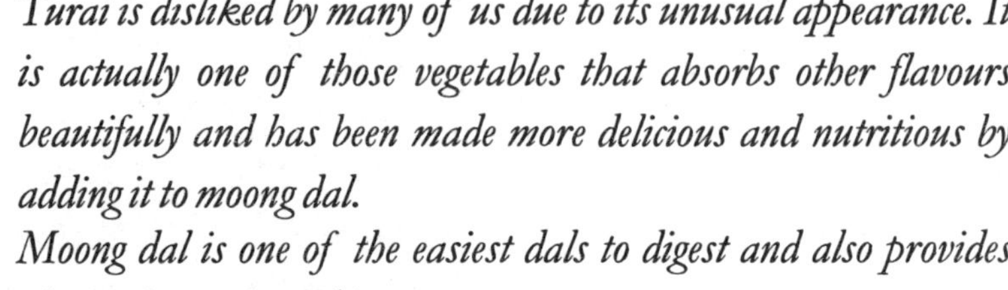

Preparation time :
15 minutes.

Cooking time :
20 minutes.

Serves 4.

Turai is disliked by many of us due to its unusual appearance. It is actually one of those vegetables that absorbs other flavours beautifully and has been made more delicious and nutritious by adding it to moong dal.
Moong dal is one of the easiest dals to digest and also provides plenty of protein and iron.

¼ cup yellow moong dal (split yellow gram)
2 cups turai (ridge gourd), peeled and chopped
¼ cup onion, finely chopped
1 teaspoon ginger-green chilli paste
¼ teaspoon turmeric powder (haldi)
¼ teaspoon cumin seeds (jeera)
a pinch asafoetida (hing)
1 teaspoon chilli powder
¼ teaspoon garam masala
1 teaspoon oil
salt to taste

For the garnish
2 tablespoons chopped coriander

1. Clean and wash the moong dal.
2. Combine the moong dal, turai, onion, ginger-green chilli paste and turmeric powder with 2 cups of water and pressure cook for 2 to 3 whistles or until the dal is cooked.

3. For the tempering, heat the oil in a non-stick pan, add the cumin seeds, asafoetida, chilli powder and garam masala and fry till the seeds crackle.
4. Pour this tempering over the prepared dal. Add salt and simmer for 5 to 7 minutes.

Serve hot, garnished with the coriander.

Nutritive values per serving :

AMT	ENERGY	PROTEIN	CHO	FAT	VIT.A	VIT.C	CALCIUM	IRON	F.ACID	FIBRE
gm	kcal	gm	gm	gm	mcg	mg	mg	mg	mcg	gm
64	56	2.7	8.2	1.4	133.9	5.1	21.5	0.6	13.8	0.4

Sambhar

Preparation time :
20 minutes.

Cooking time :
25 minutes.

Serves 6.

The aromatic flavours of this traditional South Indian dish are truly irresistible. The speciality of this sambhar is that it is made with minimal oil and loads of vegetables which enhance its nutritive value.

When served hot with Nutritious Stuffed Idlis, page 25, it makes a meal that is very hard to resist. Alternatively, relish this sambhar with steamed rice to make a wholesome meal.

For the sambhar

1 cup toovar (arhar) dal
1 onion, chopped
2 brinjals, cubed
1 drumstick, cut into 50 mm. (2") pieces
1 potato, peeled and cubed
1 tomato, finely chopped
1 tablespoon tamarind (imli) pulp
salt to taste

For the sambhar masala paste

4 to 6 red chillies, broken into pieces
1 tablespoon coriander (dhania) seeds
1 teaspoon fenugreek (methi) seeds
1 tablespoon toovar (arhar) dal
1 tablespoon split Bengal gram (chana dal)
1 tablespoon urad dal (split black lentils)
1 teaspoon turmeric powder (haldi)
½ teaspoon asafoetida (hing)

For the tempering

1 teaspoon mustard seeds (rai)
6 curry leaves
¼ teaspoon asafoetida (hing)
1 teaspoon oil

For the sambhar masala paste

1. Roast all the ingredients in a non-stick pan for 4 to 5 minutes. Allow to cool completely.
2. Grind to a fine paste in a blender using a little water. Keep aside.

How to proceed

1. Clean and wash the toovar dal.
2. Pressure cook the dal, onion, brinjals, drumstick and potato with 2 cups of water.
3. Then add the tomato, tamarind pulp, sambhar masala paste, salt and 4 cups of water and bring to a boil.
4. Prepare the tempering by heating the oil in a non-stick pan and frying the mustard seeds, curry leaves and asafoetida until the mustard seeds crackle.
5. Add to the sambhar and simmer for 10 minutes.
   Serve hot.

Nutritive values per serving :

AMT	ENERGY	PROTEIN	CHO	FAT	VIT.A	VIT.C	CALCIUM	IRON	F.ACID	FIBRE
gm	kcal	gm	gm	gm	mcg	mg	mg	mg	mcg	gm
84	146	8.3	24.8	1.5	107.9	10.4	42.4	1.2	44.4	0.9

Dhan-saak Dal

Picture on page 76

Preparation time :
25 minutes.
Cooking time :
30 minutes.
Serves 4.

A traditional Parsi dish usually prepared on Sundays for a family meal. As the name says, dhan-saak is an interesting combination of dals (dhan) and vegetables (saak) perked with loads of spices to make it a mouth-watering dish.
Being cooked only with 1 teaspoon of oil this is a really healthy recipe. We have taken care not to strain out the dal after boiling it so as to retain all the fibre and nutrients that the vegetables and dals provide. Serve the dhan-saak dal with Brown Rice, page 104, to make a completely gratifying meal.

½ cup toovar (arhar) dal
2 teaspoons yellow moong dal (split yellow gram)
2 teaspoons masoor dal (split red lentils)
2 teaspoons urad dal (split black lentils)
2 teaspoons vaal dal (split field beans)
¼ cup potato, chopped
¼ cup brinjal (baingan), chopped
¼ cup bottle gourd (doodhi / lauki), chopped
¼ cup red pumpkin (kaddu), chopped
1 spring onion (including greens), chopped
1 tablespoon fenugreek (methi) leaves, chopped
1 tomato, chopped
3 teaspoons tamarind (imli), soaked in ¼ cup of water
1 teaspoon oil
salt to taste

To be ground into a paste

1 green chilli
3 whole red chillies
4 large cloves garlic
1 stick cinnamon (dalchini)
4 cloves (laung)
25 mm. (1") piece ginger
1 cardamom (elaichi)
1 teaspoon coriander (dhania) seeds
4 peppercorns
½ teaspoon cumin seeds (jeera)
2 teaspoons chopped coriander
2 tablespoons water

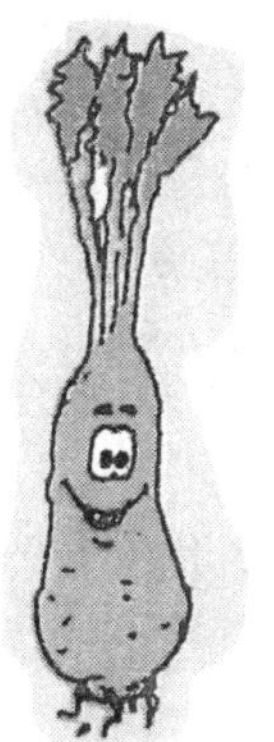

To be ground into a dry powdered masala

1 cardamom (elaichi)
1 stick cinnamon (dalchini)
1 clove (laung)

1. Clean and wash the dals.
2. Combine the dals and vegetables with 3 cups of water and and pressure cook for 3 whistles.
3. Liquidise the cooked dals and vegetables in a blender. Keep aside.
4. Heat the oil in a pan, add the prepared paste and sauté for 2 minutes.
5. Add the dal and vegetable purée, the dry powder masala, tomato, tamarind water and salt and boil for 10 to 15 minutes.
   Serve hot, with brown rice.

Nutritive values per serving :

AMT	ENERGY	PROTEIN	CHO	FAT	VIT.A	VIT.C	CALCIUM	IRON	F.ACID	FIBRE
gm	kcal	gm	gm	gm	mcg	mg	mg	mg	mcg	gm
88	127	7.2	20.5	1.8	177.3	9.4	43.9	1.2	37.8	0.8

Rice Delicacies

Vegetable Biryani

Preparation time :
15 minutes.

Cooking time :
50 minutes.

Serves 4.

Low Cal Biryani...... there could hardly be a better way to pamper your taste buds. Try this delicious biryani when you're longing for some tasty and spicy food. Cooked with minimal oil and aromatic spices, this vitamin A, iron and calcium enriched biryani is an all-in-one meal by itself.

For the rice

1 cup uncooked rice
1 clove (laung)
1 stick cinnamon (dalchini)
1 bay leaf
1 cardamom (elaichi)
salt to taste

For the vegetable gravy

1½ cups mixed boiled vegetables (carrots, peas, cauliflower, french beans, potatoes), cubed
¼ cup low fat paneer, page 144, cut into cubes
½ teaspoon cumin seeds (jeera)
¾ cup onions, finely chopped
2 teaspoons ginger-garlic paste
3 teaspoons chilli powder
2 teaspoons coriander (dhania) powder
¼ teaspoon turmeric powder (haldi)
½ teaspoon garam masala
1 cup tomatoes, chopped
½ cup low fat milk, page 142
1 teaspoon oil
salt to taste

Other ingredients

3 tablespoons low fat curds, page 143
2 tablespoons chopped coriander
a few saffron strands

For the rice

1. Clean and wash the rice.
2. In a large pan, add 3 cups of boiling water to the rice with clove, cinnamon, bay leaf, cardamom and salt.
3. Cover and simmer till the rice is nearly cooked. Drain and keep aside.

For the vegetable gravy

1. Heat the oil in a non-stick pan and add the cumin seeds.
2. When they crackle, add the onions and ginger-garlic paste and sauté till the onions turn golden brown.
3. Add the chilli powder, coriander powder, turmeric powder and garam masala with ½ cup of water and sauté for 2 to 3 minutes.
4. Add the chopped tomatoes and cook over a slow flame for 7 to 8 minutes.
5. Add the milk with ½ cup of water and continue to simmer for 5 to 7 minutes.
6. Add the boiled vegetables and paneer and mix well.

How to proceed

1. Combine the curds, coriander and saffron and mix well.
2. In a deep vessel, arrange the vegetable gravy on the base.
3. Top with the rice and spoon the curd mixture over the rice.
4. Cover with a tight lid and cook on a tava (griddle) over a slow flame for 25 to 30 minutes or bake in a pre-heated oven at 200°C (400°F) for 20 minutes. Serve hot.

Nutritive values per serving :

AMT	ENERGY	PROTEIN	CHO	FAT	VIT.A	VIT.C	CALCIUM	IRON	F.ACID	FIBRE
gm	kcal	gm	gm	gm	mcg	mg	mg	mg	mcg	gm
170	238	8.4	47.4	1.7	424.3	29.6	180.8	1.3	25.2	1.4

Masala Bhaat

Picture on facing page

Preparation time :
15 minutes.
Cooking time :
20 minutes.
Serves 4.

This traditional Maharashtrian rice is an amazing combination of spicy flavours and mouth-watering textures. When served with low fat curds, page 143, or raita it makes a complete meal in itself. Instead of brinjals and tendli, you can choose vegetables that are handy and whip up an easy nutritious meal in a jiffy.

1 cup uncooked rice
½ cup brinjals (baingan), diced
½ cup tendli, sliced vertically
a pinch asafoetida (hing)
12 mm. (½") piece ginger, grated
½ teaspoon turmeric powder (haldi)
½ teaspoon cumin seeds (jeera)
½ cup onions, chopped
2 green chillies, chopped
1 teaspoon oil
salt to taste

To be ground into a powder

½ teaspoon cumin seeds (jeera)
½ teaspoon coriander (dhania) seeds
8 to 10 peppercorns
3 cloves (laung)

1. **Masala Bhaat,** *recipe above*
2. **Mixed Veggie Raita,** *page 130*
3. **Doodhi Theplas,** *page 117*
4. **Vaal ki Usal,** *page 81*

To be mixed into a topping

¼ cup cauliflower, grated

¼ cup coriander, chopped

½ teaspoon coriander-cumin seed (dhania-jeera) powder

1 teaspoon chilli powder

½ teaspoon sugar

1. Clean, wash and soak the rice for about 10 minutes. Drain and keep aside.
2. Heat the oil in a pressure cooker and add the asafoetida, ginger, turmeric powder and cumin seeds.
3. When the seeds crackle, add the onions and green chillies and sauté till the onions turn translucent.
4. Add the brinjals, tendli and the soaked rice.
5. Add the ground powder and salt with 2½ cups of hot water and pressure cook for 2 to 3 whistles.
6. When the rice is done, add the topping mixture and toss well.
   Serve hot.

Nutritive values per serving :

AMT	ENERGY	PROTEIN	CHO	FAT	VIT.A	VIT.C	CALCIUM	IRON	F.ACID	FIBRE
gm	kcal	gm	gm	gm	mcg	mg	mg	mg	mcg	gm
96	169	3.7	35.2	1.6	130.0	11.0	22.7	0.7	9.5	0.6

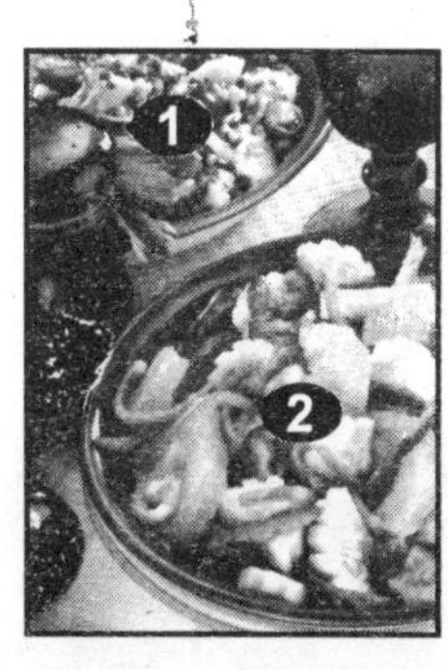

1. Minty Bean Salad, *page 125*

2. Sweet Lime and Pepper Salad, *page 129*

Brown Rice

Picture on page 76

Preparation time :
10 minutes.

Cooking time :
20 minutes.

Serves 4.

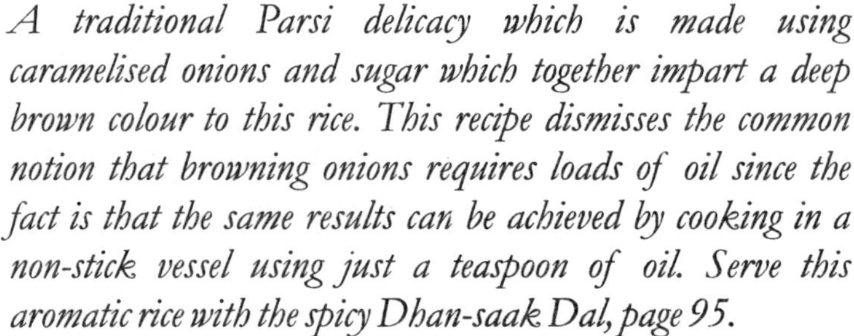

A traditional Parsi delicacy which is made using caramelised onions and sugar which together impart a deep brown colour to this rice. This recipe dismisses the common notion that browning onions requires loads of oil since the fact is that the same results can be achieved by cooking in a non-stick vessel using just a teaspoon of oil. Serve this aromatic rice with the spicy Dhan-saak Dal, page 95.

1½ cups rice
1 large onion, sliced
2 sticks cinnamon (dalchini)
2 cloves (laung)
3 cloves garlic, crushed (optional)
1 teaspoon sugar
1 teaspoon oil
salt to taste

1. Heat the oil in a non-stick pan, add the onion and sauté till the onion turns golden brown.
2. Add the cinnamon, cloves and crushed garlic and sauté for another 2 minutes.
3. Add the rice, salt and 3 cups of hot water.
4. Cover and cook over a slow flame till the rice is almost done.
5. Melt the sugar in ½ teaspoon of water over a slow flame and when it caramelises, add to the rice while it is cooking.
   Serve this rice with hot dhan-saak dal.

Nutritive values per serving :

AMT	ENERGY	PROTEIN	CHO	FAT	VIT.A	VIT.C	CALCIUM	IRON	F.ACID	FIBRE
gm	kcal	gm	gm	gm	mcg	mg	mg	mg	mcg	gm
87	235	4.4	50.8	1.6	11.3	2.7	17.6	0.6	6.3	0.3

Spicy Sprouts Pulao

Preparation time :
10 minutes.
Cooking time :
15 minutes.
Serves 4.

This spicy rice delicacy is a perfect main dish for the times when you have lots of other last minute preparations. All you have to do is to temper the rice and sprouts and let it pressure cook while you complete other chores.
Sprouts are easier to digest and abound in protein, calcium, iron as well as vitamin C. Serve with a chilled low fat raita.

1 cup uncooked rice
1 cup mixed sprouts (moath beans, red chana, moong etc.)
1 bay leaf
1 clove (laung)
1 stick cinnamon (dalchini)
½ teaspoon cumin seeds (jeera)
1 onion, finely chopped
1 teaspoon ginger-green chilli paste
¼ teaspoon turmeric powder (haldi)
1 teaspoon chilli powder
1 teaspoon coriander-cumin seed (dhania-jeera) powder
1 teaspoon oil
salt to taste

For the garnish
2 tablespoons chopped coriander

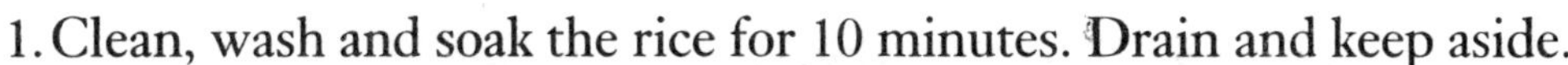

1. Clean, wash and soak the rice for 10 minutes. Drain and keep aside.
2. Heat the oil in a pressure cooker and add the bay leaf, clove, cinnamon and cumin seeds.
3. When the seeds crackle, add the onion and ginger-green chilli paste and sauté till the onion turns translucent.
4. Add the rice and sprouts and sauté for 2 minutes.

5. Add the turmeric powder, chilli powder, coriander-cumin seed powder and salt with 2½ cups of hot water. Pressure cook for 2 whistles.
Serve hot, garnished with the coriander.

Nutritive values per serving :

AMT	ENERGY	PROTEIN	CHO	FAT	VIT.A	VIT.C	CALCIUM	IRON	F.ACID	FIBRE
gm	kcal	gm	gm	gm	mcg	mg	mg	mg	mcg	gm
79	216	6.4	43.1	2.0	132.5	4.5	45.3	1.4	16.9	0.9

Lemon Rice

Preparation time :
5 minutes.
Cooking time :
10 minutes.
Serves 4.

This dish is ideal for the summer. Keep in mind the fact that the lemon juice has to be added judiciously to suit your palate so that you do not end up with a "khatta" or bland rice. I enjoy this dish with Rasam, page 89, or just a bowl of salad. The lemon in the rice aids in the absorption of iron in your body due to its high vitamin C content.
If you have eaten a heavy breakfast, then this is a perfect dish for a light lunch.

1½ cups cooked rice
2 whole red chillies, broken into pieces
½ teaspoon mustard seeds (rai)
½ teaspoon urad dal (split black lentils)
½ teaspoon ginger, grated
1 teaspoon roasted chana dal (daria)
4 to 5 curry leaves
⅛ teaspoon turmeric powder (haldi)
juice of ½ lemon
1 teaspoon oil
salt to taste

For the garnish

1 tablespoon chopped coriander

1. Heat the oil in a non-stick pan and add the red chilies, mustard seeds, urad dal, ginger, chana dal and curry leaves.
2. When the seeds crackle, add the turmeric powder, rice, lemon juice and salt and toss well.

Serve hot, garnished with the coriander.

Nutritive values per serving :

AMT	ENERGY	PROTEIN	CHO	FAT	VIT.A	VIT.C	CALCIUM	IRON	F.ACID	FIBRE
gm	kcal	gm	gm	gm	mcg	mg	mg	mg	mcg	gm
28	90	1.9	17.3	1.5	65.3	2.5	7.6	0.3	4.5	0.1

Soya Mutter Pulao

Preparation time :
10 minutes.
Cooking time :
20 minutes.

Serves 4.

Pulaos are always a welcome addition to any meal. A pulao can often make a complete meal by itself. The soya chunks added to this aromatic pulao are easily available in the market and are a rich source of protein and vitamin B_{12}— a vitamin which is otherwise lacking in vegetarian diets.

1 cup uncooked rice
¼ cup soya nuggets (chunks)
¼ cup green peas
½ teaspoon cumin seeds (jeera)
1 stick cinnamon (dalchini)
2 cloves (laung)
1 bay leaf
1 cardamom (elaichi)
½ cup onions, chopped
¼ teaspoon turmeric powder (haldi)

¼ teaspoon garam masala
1 teaspoon coriander (dhania) powder
½ cup tomatoes, chopped
1 teaspoon oil
salt to taste

To be ground into a chilli-garlic paste
3 cloves garlic
3 whole red chillies

1. Clean, wash and soak the rice for 10 minutes. Drain and keep aside.
2. Combine the soya nuggets and salt with 1 cup of water and pressure cook for 2 whistles. Drain and keep aside.
3. Heat the oil in a pressure cooker and add the cumin seeds, cinnamon, cloves, bay leaf and cardamom.
4. When the seeds crackle, add the onions and prepared chilli-garlic paste and sauté till the onions turn golden brown.
5. Add the turmeric powder, garam masala, coriander powder, tomatoes, rice, green peas, cooked soya nuggets and salt and sauté for another 2 minutes.
6. Add 2 cups of hot water and pressure cook for 2 whistles.
   Serve hot.

Nutritive values per serving :

AMT	ENERGY	PROTEIN	CHO	FAT	VIT.A	VIT.C	CALCIUM	IRON	F.ACID	FIBRE
gm	kcal	gm	gm	gm	mcg	mg	mg	mg	mcg	gm
89	184	5.1	35.9	2.1	100.8	7.9	30.6	1.0	14.1	0.8

Crispy Rotis and Parathas

Methi Makai ki Roti

Preparation time :
10 minutes.

Cooking time :
15 minutes.

Makes 6 rotis.

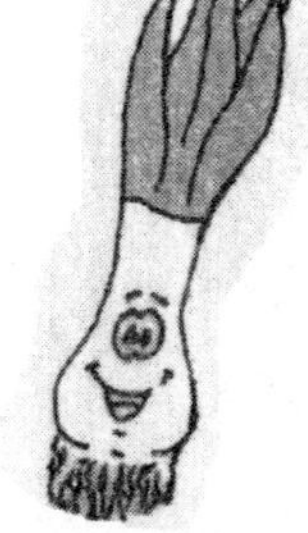

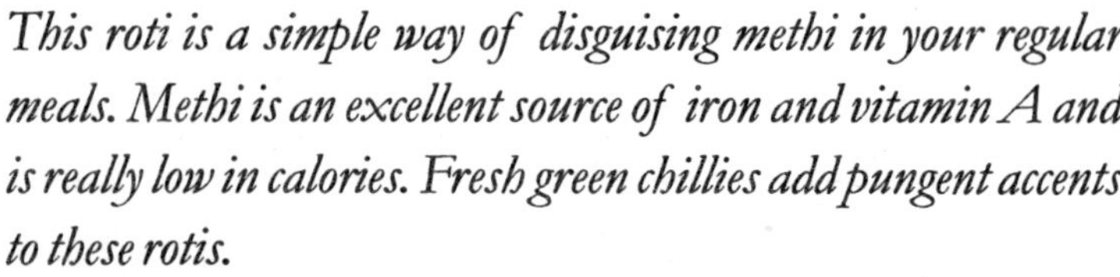

This roti is a simple way of disguising methi in your regular meals. Methi is an excellent source of iron and vitamin A and is really low in calories. Fresh green chillies add pungent accents to these rotis.

1 cup maize flour (makai ka atta)
2 tablespoons whole wheat flour (gehun ka atta)
½ cup fenugreek (methi) leaves, chopped
1 green chilli, finely chopped
salt to taste

Other ingredients

1 teaspoon oil for cooking

1. Combine all the ingredients and knead into a soft dough using enough warm water. Knead well.
2. Divide the dough into 6 equal parts.
3. Roll out each portion between two sheets of plastic into a circle of 100 mm. (4") diameter.
4. Cook the rotis on a hot non-stick tava (griddle) on both sides using very little oil till brown spots appear.
   Serve hot.

Nutritive values per roti :

AMT	ENERGY	PROTEIN	CHO	FAT	VIT.A	VIT.C	CALCIUM	IRON	F.ACID	FIBRE
gm	kcal	gm	gm	gm	mcg	mg	mg	mg	mcg	gm
22	38	1.2	6.1	1.0	68.0	2.2	12.1	0.4	1.1	0.4

Palak aur Chawal ki Roti

Preparation time :
15 minutes.
Cooking time :
20 minutes.
Makes 6 rotis.

These soft rotis are best served with a thick dal or a subji. You can use other leafy vegetables or a combination of leafy vegetables like methi, mint etc. to enhance the nutritional value of these rotis.

½ cup rice flour (chawal ka atta)
⅓ cup cooked rice
¼ cup spinach (palak), blanched and drained
salt to taste

1. Blend the cooked rice and spinach to a smooth purée in a blender without adding water.
2. Combine the prepared purée, rice flour, salt and enough water to make a soft dough. Knead well.
3. Divide the dough into 6 equal parts and roll out each portion into a thin circle of 150 mm. (6") diameter, using flour to roll the rotis.
4. Cook one side of a roti on a tava (griddle) and put the other side directly over a gas flame for a few seconds till the roti puffs up and has brown spots on the surface.

Serve hot.

Nutritive values per roti :

AMT	ENERGY	PROTEIN	CHO	FAT	VIT.A	VIT.C	CALCIUM	IRON	F.ACID	FIBRE
gm	kcal	gm	gm	gm	mcg	mg	mg	mg	mcg	gm
27	47	1.1	10.3	0.2	790.5	4.0	11.6	0.3	18.4	0.1

Saatdhan Parathas

Picture on page 127

Preparation time :
10 minutes.
Cooking time :
15 minutes.
Makes *10 parathas.*

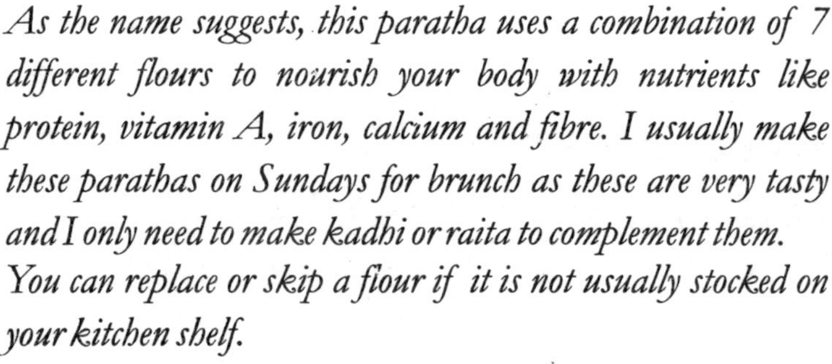

As the name suggests, this paratha uses a combination of 7 different flours to nourish your body with nutrients like protein, vitamin A, iron, calcium and fibre. I usually make these parathas on Sundays for brunch as these are very tasty and I only need to make kadhi or raita to complement them. You can replace or skip a flour if it is not usually stocked on your kitchen shelf.

3 tablespoons whole wheat flour (gehun ka atta)
3 tablespoons jowar flour (white millet flour)
3 tablespoons bajra flour (black millet flour)
3 tablespoons ragi (nachni) flour
2 tablespoons Bengal gram flour (besan)
3 tablespoons maize flour (makai ka atta)
2 tablespoons rice flour (chawal ka atta)
1 teaspoon garlic paste
$\frac{1}{2}$ teaspoon turmeric powder (haldi)
$1\frac{1}{2}$ teaspoons chilli powder
$\frac{1}{2}$ cup bottle gourd (doodhi / lauki), grated
$\frac{1}{2}$ cup carrots, grated
1 tablespoon chopped coriander
4 tablespoons low fat curds, page 143
1 teaspoon oil
salt to taste

1. Combine all the ingredients and knead into a soft dough, using water if required.
2. Divide the dough into 10 equal portions.
3. Roll out each portion into a circle of 125 mm. (5") diameter using flour to roll the paratha.
4. Cook each paratha over a tava (griddle) till both sides are golden brown in colour.

   Serve hot.

Nutritive values per paratha :

AMT	ENERGY	PROTEIN	CHO	FAT	VIT.A	VIT.C	CALCIUM	IRON	F.ACID	FIBRE
gm	kcal	gm	gm	gm	mcg	mg	mg	mg	mcg	gm
25	56	1.8	10.3	0.9	116.9	0.7	24.6	0.7	6.0	0.3

Nutritious Garlic Naans

Preparation time :
50 minutes.

Cooking time :
15 minutes.

Makes 8 naans.

Try these whole wheat flour naans and believe me you will never again be tempted to eat unhealthy plain flour (maida) naans which we all have been eating.
Garlic due to its dominant flavour is usually omitted in many dishes but when combined with soya and wheat flour, it is transformed into a delicacy. This aromatic herb has many medicinal values, one of them being to lower the blood cholesterol levels in your body.
Soya, the other ingredient used in these naans, is the prime source of protein and vitamin B_{12} *in a vegetarian diet.*

1 cup whole wheat flour (gehun ka atta)
¼ cup soya flour
¼ cup low fat curds, page 143
⅛ teaspoon soda bi-carb
1 tablespoon garlic, finely chopped
1 teaspoon oil
½ teaspoon salt

1. Combine all the ingredients and knead into a soft dough using enough water. Knead well (approx. 4 to 5 minutes).
2. Cover the dough with a wet muslin cloth and leave aside for 45 minutes.
3. Divide the dough into 8 equal portions and roll out each portion into a circle of 100 mm. (4") diameter.

4. Grease the insides of a pressure cooker very lightly with oil. Remove the lid of the pressure cooker and heat it upside down over an open flame.
5. Apply a little water on one side of each naan and stick the wet side of the naan around the inside of the pressure cooker.
6. Cook till brown spots appear and the naan peels away easily from the sides of the pressure cooker. You can stick 3 to 4 naans at a time on the inside of the pressure cooker.

Serve hot.

Nutritive values per naan :

AMT	ENERGY	PROTEIN	CHO	FAT	VIT.A	VIT.C	CALCIUM	IRON	F.ACID	FIBRE
gm	kcal	gm	gm	gm	mcg	mg	mg	mg	mcg	gm
17	63	2.8	10.1	1.3	18.6	0.0	20.1	0.9	7.0	0.3

Lazeez Parathas

Preparation time :
10 minutes.
Cooking time :
15 to 20 minutes.
Makes 10 parathas.

Chana dal and broken wheat make unusual beginnings for a paratha. This combination of Bengal gram dal (pulse) and broken wheat (cereal) forms a complete source of protein and also provides fibre. Apart from being rich in nutrients, these parathas are also rich in taste and flavour.
Serve them hot and fresh, as re-heating these parathas is not a good idea!

¼ cup broken wheat (dalia)
1 tablespoon split Bengal gram (chana dal)
1 cup whole wheat flour (gehun ka atta)
1 teaspoon ginger-green chilli paste
4 tablespoons chopped coriander
salt to taste

Other ingredients
1 teaspoon oil for cooking

1. Wash the chana dal and broken wheat and pressure cook in 1½ cups of water for 3 whistles. Allow to cool completely.
2. Add the remaining ingredients and knead into a soft dough using water only if required.
3. Divide the dough into 10 equal portions and roll each portion into a circle of 125 mm. (5") diameter.
4. Cook each paratha on a non-stick tava (griddle) using a dash of oil till it is lightly browned on both sides.

   Serve hot, with low fat curds.

Nutritive values per paratha :

AMT	ENERGY	PROTEIN	CHO	FAT	VIT.A	VIT.C	CALCIUM	IRON	F.ACID	FIBRE
gm	kcal	gm	gm	gm	mcg	mg	mg	mg	mcg	gm
18	61	2.0	11.4	0.8	92.7	1.6	9.7	0.8	6.2	0.3

Methi Paneer Parathas

Preparation time :
10 minutes.
Cooking time :
20 minutes.
Makes 4 parathas.

A yummy variation to paneer parathas ..... I have added methi to these parathas as it provides substantial amounts of vitamin A and iron. Relish these parathas with low fat curds, page 143 or dal.

For the dough

¾ cup whole wheat flour (gehun ka atta)
salt to taste

For the methi paneer stuffing

½ cup fenugreek (methi) leaves, finely chopped
½ cup low fat paneer, page 144, grated
½ teaspoon cumin seeds (jeera)
½ teaspoon ginger-green chilli paste

1/8 teaspoon turmeric powder (haldi)
1 teaspoon oil
salt to taste

For the dough

1. Combine the wheat flour and salt and knead into a soft dough, using enough water. Knead well.
2. Cover the dough with a wet muslin cloth and leave aside for 10 minutes.
3. Divide the dough into 4 equal portions.

For the methi paneer stuffing

1. Heat the oil in a non-stick pan and add the cumin seeds and ginger-green chilli paste.
2. When the seeds crackle, add the fenugreek leaves, turmeric powder and salt and sauté for 2 to 3 minutes.
3. Add the paneer and mix well. Divide the stuffing into 4 equal portions. Keep aside.

How to proceed

1. Roll out one portion of the dough into a circle of 75 mm. (3") diameter.
2. Place one portion of the methi paneer stuffing in the centre of the circle.
3. Bring together all the sides in the centre and seal tightly.
4. Roll out again into a circle of 125 mm. (5") diameter using flour to roll the paratha.
5. Cook on a non-stick tava (griddle) until both sides are golden brown.
6. Repeat with the remaining dough and stuffing to make 3 more parathas. Serve hot.

Nutritive values per paratha :

AMT	ENERGY	PROTEIN	CHO	FAT	VIT.A	VIT.C	CALCIUM	IRON	F.ACID	FIBRE
gm	kcal	gm	gm	gm	mcg	mg	mg	mg	mcg	gm
33	109	5.5	18.1	1.6	99.0	2.2	126.3	1.2	7.2	0.4

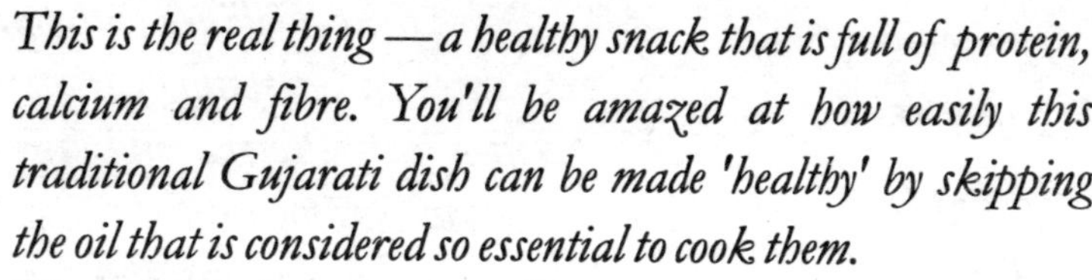

Doodhi Theplas

Picture on page 101

Preparation time :
5 minutes.
Cooking time :
25 minutes.
Makes 15 theplas.

This is the real thing — a healthy snack that is full of protein, calcium and fibre. You'll be amazed at how easily this traditional Gujarati dish can be made 'healthy' by skipping the oil that is considered so essential to cook them.
They also make a great travelling snack, as they stay well for a couple of days without refrigeration and also beautifully complement a cup of hot masala tea.

2 cups whole wheat flour (gehun ka atta)
¾ cup bottle gourd (doodhi / lauki), grated
½ cup low fat curds, page 143
½ teaspoon turmeric powder (haldi)
1½ teaspoons chilli powder
1 teaspoon oil
salt to taste

1. Mix all the ingredients and knead into a soft dough using water only if required.
2. Divide the dough into 15 equal portions.
3. Roll out each portion thinly into a circle of 125 mm. (5") diameter.
4. Cook each thepla on both sides on a non-stick pan until brown spots appear on the surface.
   Serve hot.

Nutritive values per thepla :

AMT	ENERGY	PROTEIN	CHO	FAT	VIT.A	VIT.C	CALCIUM	IRON	F.ACID	FIBRE
gm	kcal	gm	gm	gm	mcg	mg	mg	mg	mcg	gm
20	55	2.0	10.5	0.6	7.2	0.0	17.0	0.7	5.2	0.3

Bajra Kand Rotis

Preparation time :
15 minutes.
Cooking time :
15 minutes.
Makes 7 rotis.

Bajra flour combined with purple yam, curds and garlic paste makes an interesting variation to plain bajra rotis which we often eat. Protein and iron are two important nutrients provided by these rotis.
Like all bajra rotis, they tend to get chewy if they are served cold without a brushing of ghee. So serve these hot to avoid the use of ghee or butter for brushing.

1 cup bajra flour (black millet flour)
½ cup kand (purple yam), boiled, peeled and grated
¼ cup low fat curds, page 143
½ teaspoon garlic paste
½ teaspoon ginger-green chilli paste
½ teaspoon fennel seeds (saunf)
1 teaspoon oil
salt to taste

1. Combine all the ingredients and knead into a soft dough using water only if required.
2. Divide the dough into 7 equal portions.
3. Roll out each portion into a circle of 125 mm. (5") diameter.
4. Cook each roti on a tava (griddle) on both sides till brown spots appear. Serve hot.

Nutritive values per roti :

AMT	ENERGY	PROTEIN	CHO	FAT	VIT.A	VIT.C	CALCIUM	IRON	F.ACID	FIBRE
gm	kcal	gm	gm	gm	mcg	mg	mg	mg	mcg	gm
24	69	2.0	12.0	1.4	31.8	0.0	18.8	1.2	7.9	0.3

Tangy Salads and Raitas

Lauki aur Phudine ka Raita

Preparation time :
5 minutes.
Cooking time :
5 minutes.
Serves 4.

This tangy curd preparation makes a wonderful summertime treat when served chilled. Grated lauki contributes minimal calories and also blends perfectly with the 'minty' flavour of this raita.
If you are fussy about milk, this raita is an ideal meal time feast to meet your protein and calcium requirements.

1 cup bottle gourd (doodhi / lauki), grated
1 cup low fat curds, page 143, beaten
4 tablespoons chopped mint (phudina)
¼ teaspoon roasted cumin seeds (jeera)
¼ teaspoon black salt (sanchal)
½ teaspoon sugar
salt to taste

1. Steam the bottle gourd for 4 to 5 minutes. Allow to cool completely.
2. Combine all the ingredients in a serving bowl and whisk well. Serve chilled.

Nutritive values per serving :

AMT	ENERGY	PROTEIN	CHO	FAT	VIT.A	VIT.C	CALCIUM	IRON	F.ACID	FIBRE
gm	kcal	gm	gm	gm	mcg	mg	mg	mg	mcg	gm
34	25	2.1	4.0	0.1	64.8	1.3	81.4	0.8	4.6	0.2

Barley and Corn Kachumber

Preparation time :
5 minutes.
Cooking time :
10 minutes.
Serves 4.

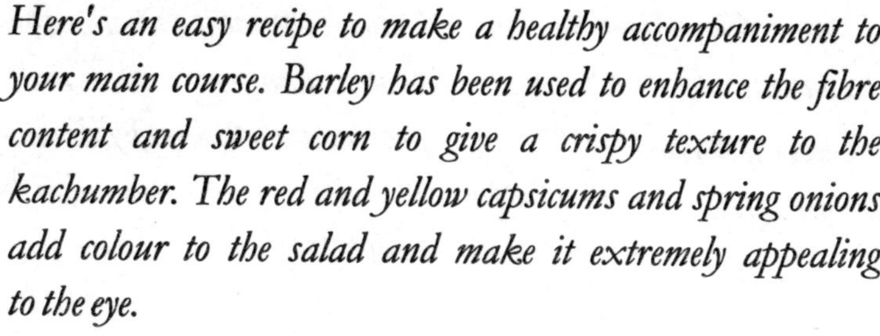

Here's an easy recipe to make a healthy accompaniment to your main course. Barley has been used to enhance the fibre content and sweet corn to give a crispy texture to the kachumber. The red and yellow capsicums and spring onions add colour to the salad and make it extremely appealing to the eye.

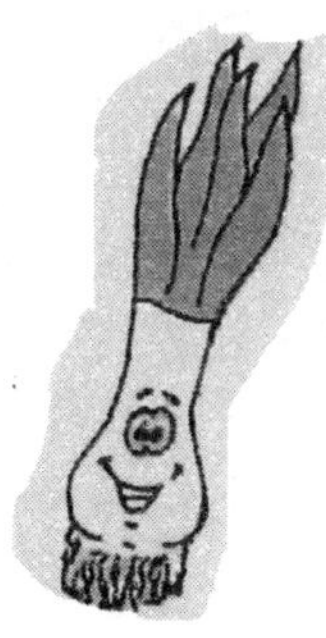

¼ cup barley (jau)
⅓ cup sweet corn
½ cup red and yellow capsicum, chopped
1 spring onion (including greens), chopped
2 tablespoons chopped coriander
1 teaspoon lemon juice
½ teaspoon sugar
½ teaspoon roasted cumin seed (jeera) powder
salt to taste

1. Pressure cook the barley and corn with 1 cup of water for 2 whistles. Drain and allow to cool completely.
2. Combine all the ingredients for the salad in a serving bowl and toss well. Chill for at least 2 hours before serving.

Handy Tip *The discarded barley water can be used for vegetable gravies and dals as it is rich in water-soluble vitamins like B and C.*

Nutritive values per serving :

AMT	ENERGY	PROTEIN	CHO	FAT	VIT.A	VIT.C	CALCIUM	IRON	F.ACID	FIBRE
gm	kcal	gm	gm	gm	mcg	mg	mg	mg	mcg	gm
50	53	1.9	10.8	0.3	207.4	29.7	16.1	0.6	1.6	1.0

Chick Pea Salad with Mint Dressing

Preparation time :
15 minutes.
Cooking time :
20 minutes.
Serves 4.

One of the most nutritious beans — chick peas are rich in iron, protein and folic acid. Curds enrich this tangy salad with more protein and calcium while coriander and mint increase its vitamin A content. Chill this salad before you serve it so as to relish its delightful flavours.

1 cup chick peas (kabuli chana), soaked overnight
2 firm tomatoes, cubed
4 spring onions (including greens), sliced
1 cup cucumber, diced
salt to taste

For the mint dressing

½ cup chopped mint (phudina) leaves
½ cup chopped coriander
2 tablespoons low fat curds, page 143
½ teaspoon sugar
salt and pepper to taste

For the dressing

Combine all the ingredients and blend into a smooth purée in a blender. Refrigerate.

For the salad

1. Drain and wash the soaked chick peas. Add fresh water and salt and pressure cook the chick peas for 3 to 4 whistles till they are soft. Cool completely.
2. Combine the chick peas with the remaining ingredients for the salad.
3. Add the dressing and mix well.

   Serve chilled.

Nutritive values per serving :

AMT	ENERGY	PROTEIN	CHO	FAT	VIT.A	VIT.C	CALCIUM	IRON	F.ACID	FIBRE
gm	kcal	gm	gm	gm	mcg	mg	mg	mg	mcg	gm
142	105	5.4	18.6	1.3	592.0	39.7	115.3	2.9	64.8	2.5

Pineapple Cucumber Salad

Picture on page 127

Preparation time :
5 minutes.
No Cooking.
Serves 4.

Pineapple and cucumbers tossed with coriander and lemon juice furnish a storehouse of vitamin C which is extremely essential to build up your immunity against infections. Honey imparts a delicate sweetness to this tangy salad. Rather than serving it as an occasional treat, make this sweet and sour salad a part of your daily meal and say goodbye to infections!

1 cup pineapple, cut into small pieces
1 cup cucumber, cut into small pieces
6 cherry tomatoes, halved
½ cup lettuce, torn into pieces
2 tablespoons chopped coriander
2 tablespoons lemon juice
1 teaspoon honey
1½ tablespoons roasted chana dal (daria), coarsely powdered
salt and freshly ground pepper to taste

1. In a bowl, combine the lemon juice, honey, chana dal powder, salt and pepper and mix well.
2. Add the rest of the ingredients and toss lightly.
   Serve immediately.

Nutritive values per serving :

AMT	ENERGY	PROTEIN	CHO	FAT	VIT.A	VIT.C	CALCIUM	IRON	F.ACID	FIBRE
gm	kcal	gm	gm	gm	mcg	mg	mg	mg	mcg	gm
143	69	2.4	13.5	0.7	409.1	35.4	51.5	2.2	21.3	1.0

Crunchy Vegetable Salad

Preparation time :
10 minutes.
No Cooking.
Serves 4.

A colourful salad that is difficult to resist. The orange and lemon dressing adds a cooling and refreshing flavour which also increases the vitamin C content of the salad. Feel free to choose any combination of crunchy vegetables you like.

1/2 cup red cabbage, shredded
1/2 cup cabbage, shredded
1/2 cup carrots, thinly sliced
1/2 cup white radish (mooli), thinly sliced
1/4 cup capsicum, thinly sliced

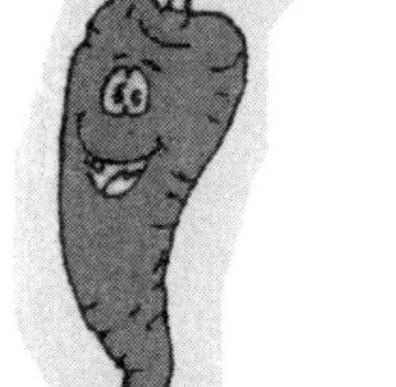

1 tablespoon honey
2 tablespoons orange juice
1/8 teaspoon prepared mustard
1 teaspoon lemon juice
salt and pepper to taste

1. Combine all the ingredients in a salad bowl and refrigerate.
2. Add the dressing to the salad just before serving and toss well. Serve chilled.

Nutritive values per serving :

AMT	ENERGY	PROTEIN	CHO	FAT	VIT.A	VIT.C	CALCIUM	IRON	F.ACID	FIBRE
gm	kcal	gm	gm	gm	mcg	mg	mg	mg	mcg	gm
76	37	1.0	8.6	0.1	418.8	41.7	33.7	0.5	7.2	0.7

Spicy Kachumber

Picture on page 76

Preparation time : 10 minutes.

No Cooking.

Serves 4.

A chatpata salad spiked with cumin and chilli powder. Vitamins A and C are the two important nutrients provided by this spicy kachumber. Serve it chilled with Dhan-saak Dal, page 95, and Brown Rice, page 104, to complete a full meal on a lazy afternoon.

1 cup sliced onions
1 cup cucumber, thinly sliced
½ cup sliced tomatoes
½ teaspoon roasted cumin seed (jeera) powder
¼ teaspoon chilli powder
juice of ½ lemon
salt to taste

Combine all the ingredients in a serving bowl and refrigerate.
Serve chilled.

Nutritive values per serving :

AMT	ENERGY	PROTEIN	CHO	FAT	VIT.A	VIT.C	CALCIUM	IRON	F.ACID	FIBRE
gm	kcal	gm	gm	gm	mcg	mg	mg	mg	mcg	gm
62	16	0.5	3.3	0.1	50.9	9.1	19.5	0.4	9.5	0.4

Minty Bean Salad

Picture on page 102

Preparation time : 15 minutes.

Cooking time : 10 minutes.

Serves 4.

For an accompaniment to a main dish, try this novel combination of black-eyed beans (lobhia) with a fresh minty flavour. Tomato, coriander and lemon add more tang and nutritional value i.e. vitamin A, vitamin C, folic acid and iron to this salad.
Serve at room temperature immediately after tossing it or refrigerate until chilled.

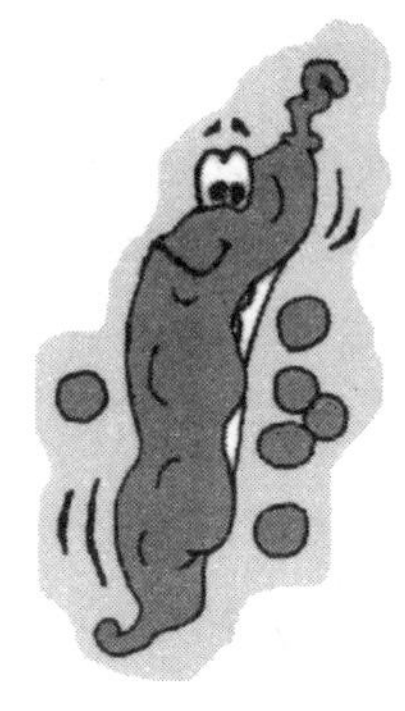

½ cup black eyed beans (lobhia), soaked overnight
1 onion, finely chopped
1 tomato, finely chopped
1 cucumber, peeled and chopped
2 tablespoons chopped coriander
2 tablespoons chopped mint (phudina)
½ green chilli, finely chopped (optional)
juice of ½ lemon
¼ teaspoon black salt (sanchal)
salt to taste

1. Combine the beans and salt and pressure cook for 3 to 4 whistles until they are cooked and soft. Drain and allow to cool completely.
2. Combine all the ingredients (including the beans) in a serving bowl and mix well.

Serve chilled.

You can use halved cherry tomatoes in the above recipe as shown in the picture on page 102.

Nutritive values per serving :

AMT	ENERGY	PROTEIN	CHO	FAT	VIT.A	VIT.C	CALCIUM	IRON	F.ACID	FIBRE
gm	kcal	gm	gm	gm	mcg	mg	mg	mg	mcg	gm
83	53	3.1	9.6	0.2	205.8	13.3	38.3	1.6	26.4	0.9

1. Radish Koftas in Kadhi, *page 84*
2. Saatdhan Parathas, *page 112*
3. Pineapple Cucumber Salad, *page 123*

Sweet Lime and Pepper Salad

Picture on page 102

Preparation time :
10 minutes.
No Cooking.
Serves 3.

Simple, quick and easy, this salad can be prepared in minutes. Capsicum is a much ignored salad vegetable that has been combined with lots of colours and flavours which perfectly complements the delicate flavour of sweet lime.

This salad is a great accompaniment for a continental main course and is also a good choice for takeaway lunches. To keep salad fresh and crisp, add salt just before you eat it. This is because salt in a salad draws out all the water from the vegetables and leaves them limp.

1 cup sweet lime segments
1 cup yellow, red and green capsicum, sliced
2 cups lettuce, torn into pieces
1 cup cucumber, sliced

To be mixed into a dressing

½ teaspoon mustard (rai) powder
½ teaspoon pepper powder
juice of 1 lemon
salt to taste

1. Low Fat Kulfi with Strawberry Sauce, *page 136*
2. Pineapple Basundi, *page 132*

1. Combine all the ingredients for the salad in a bowl and chill.
2. Just before serving, pour the dressing over the salad and toss well. Serve immediately.

Nutritive values per serving :

AMT	ENERGY	PROTEIN	CHO	FAT	VIT.A	VIT.C	CALCIUM	IRON	F.ACID	FIBRE
gm	kcal	gm	gm	gm	mcg	mg	mg	mg	mcg	gm
257	68	3.5	12.0	0.7	1229.6	102.5	92.0	3.5	6.1	1.6

Mixed Veggie Raita

Picture on page 101

Preparation time :
10 minutes.
No Cooking.
Serves 4.

This hearty curd preparation is filled with colour, flavour and nutritional goodness. The low fat curds provide the much needed essential nutrients like calcium and protein. Serve chilled to relish all the flavours.

1 cup low fat curds, page 143, beaten
½ cup beetroot, boiled and cubed
1 small cucumber, cut into cubes
1 tomato, deseeded and chopped
1 tablespoon chopped coriander
¼ teaspoon roasted cumin seed (jeera) powder
salt to taste

Combine all the ingredients in a bowl and mix well.
Serve chilled.

Nutritive values per serving :

AMT	ENERGY	PROTEIN	CHO	FAT	VIT.A	VIT.C	CALCIUM	IRON	F.ACID	FIBRE
gm	kcal	gm	gm	gm	mcg	mg	mg	mg	mcg	gm
61	29	2.4	4.8	0.1	120.3	9.3	83.5	0.5	9.7	0.4

Delectable Mithais

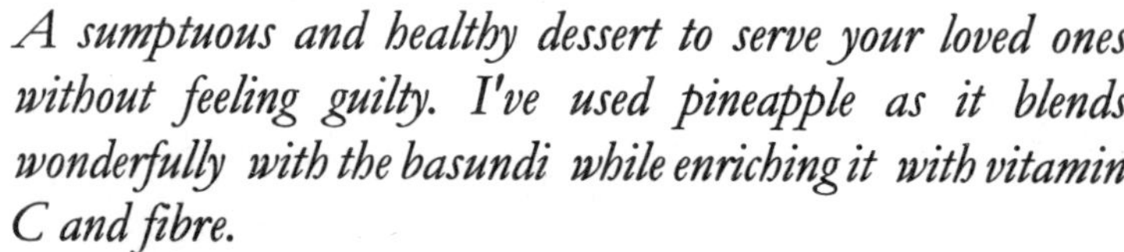

Pineapple Basundi

Picture on page 128

Preparation time :
15 minutes.
Cooking time :
40 minutes.
Serves 4.

A sumptuous and healthy dessert to serve your loved ones without feeling guilty. I've used pineapple as it blends wonderfully with the basundi while enriching it with vitamin C and fibre.
It's important to remember to use a fully ripe pineapple because an unripe fruit will require a lot more sugar thus adding on unnecessary calories.

2½ cups (500 ml.) low fat milk, page 142
¾ cup fresh pineapple, grated
5 teaspoons sugar
a few saffron strands
¼ teaspoon cardamom (elaichi) powder

For the garnish

¼ cup pineapple, cut into small pieces

1. In a small bowl, soak the saffron in a little warm milk and keep aside.
2. Put the milk in a broad non-stick pan and bring to a boil. Simmer over a medium flame stirring continuously till the milk reduces to half original quantity (approx. 250 ml.).
3. Add the saffron mixture and cardamom powder and mix well. Cool and refrigerate.
4. Combine the pineapple and sugar in a non-stick pan and cook for 5 to 6 minutes while stirring continuously till the sugar has dissolved. Allow to cool completely.
5. Add the cooled pineapple mixture to the chilled thickened milk and mix well. Serve chilled, garnished with the pineapple pieces.

Nutritive values per serving :

AMT	ENERGY	PROTEIN	CHO	FAT	VIT.A	VIT.C	CALCIUM	IRON	F.ACID	FIBRE
gm	kcal	gm	gm	gm	mcg	mg	mg	mg	mcg	gm
64	90	4.9	17.4	0.1	8.1	18.2	180.3	1.3	0.0	0.2

Sevaiiyan

Preparation time :
10 minutes.
Cooking time :
25 minutes.
Serves 4.

If you have a sweet tooth and crave for desserts after a meal, here's a fast and healthy sweet. This nutritious version of the traditional recipe of sevaiiyan skips the use of full fat milk, condensed milk and dry fruits. The vermicelli thickens the milk effortlessly to create a creamy concoction that's sure to appease your craving. A touch of cardamom powder and saffron adds colour and flavour to this traditional calcium and protein rich dish.

½ cup crushed vermicelli (sevaiiyan)
3 cups low fat milk, page 142
2 teaspoons low fat milk powder
5 teaspoons sugar
¼ teaspoon cardamom (elaichi) powder
a few saffron strands

1. Heat a non-stick pan, add the vermicelli and cook over a slow flame till it is golden brown, while stirring occasionally.
2. Add the milk and simmer till the milk reduces to half its original quantity (for approx. 15 to 20 minutes).
3. Add the milk powder, sugar, cardamom powder and saffron and mix well. Serve warm.

Nutritive values per serving :

AMT	ENERGY	PROTEIN	CHO	FAT	VIT.A	VIT.C	CALCIUM	IRON	F.ACID	FIBRE
gm	kcal	gm	gm	gm	mcg	mg	mg	mg	mcg	gm
26	95	6.1	17.4	0.0	0.0	0.8	206.9	0.3	0.0	0.0

Fruit Sandesh

Preparation time :
5 minutes.
Cooking time :
5 minutes.
Serves 4.

Sandesh is a classic Bengali sweet made with fresh paneer or chenna which is flavoured in a variety of ways. Here I have used a fascinating combination of calcium rich low fat paneer and vitamin C rich fruits — oranges and strawberries to make an attractive festive delicacy.

For the sandesh

1 recipe low fat paneer, page 144
4 teaspoons sugar
2 teaspoons low fat milk powder
1 tablespoon low fat milk, page 142

For the garnish

1/4 cup chopped fresh fruits (oranges, strawberries etc.)

For the orange sauce

1/3 cup fresh orange juice
1/4 teaspoon cornflour
1 teaspoon sugar
2 to 3 drops lemon juice

For the sandesh

1. Combine all the ingredients and blend to a smooth paste in a blender.
2. Spread the sandesh evenly in a 100 mm. (4") diameter serving dish and chill for at least 30 minutes.

For the orange sauce

1. Combine all the ingredients in a pan and mix well.
2. Cook till the sugar has dissolved. Cool completely.

How to proceed

1. Garnish the sandesh with the chopped fruits.
2. Cut the sandesh into squares and serve with the orange sauce.

Nutritive values per serving :

AMT	ENERGY	PROTEIN	CHO	FAT	VIT.A	VIT.C	CALCIUM	IRON	F.ACID	FIBRE
gm	kcal	gm	gm	gm	mcg	mg	mg	mg	mcg	gm
47	93	6.1	16.9	0.1	216.2	9.3	220.9	0.4	0.0	0.1

Low Fat Kulfi with Strawberry Sauce

Picture on page 128

Preparation time : 10 minutes.

Cooking time : 40 minutes.

Serves 6.

Kulfi is a frozen dessert which all of us relish but often tend to avoid because of its high calorific value. Here is a simple yummy low fat kulfi that doesn't take forever to prepare and provides substantial amounts of calcium without the fat. Enhance its appeal and vitamin C levels by serving it with strawberry sauce.

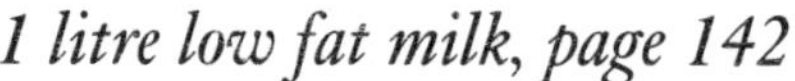

1 litre low fat milk, page 142
1 teaspoon cornflour
6 teaspoons sugar
a few saffron strands
¼ teaspoon cardamom (elaichi) powder

To be mixed together for the strawberry sauce

½ cup strawberries, crushed
4 teaspoons powdered sugar

1. In a small bowl, soak the saffron in a little warm milk and keep aside.
2. Dissolve the cornflour in 1 tablespoon of milk and keep aside.
3. Put the milk in a broad non-stick pan and bring to a boil. Simmer over a medium flame stirring continuously till the milk reduces to little more than half the original quantity (approx. 600 ml.).
4. Add the cornflour solution and sugar and bring to a boil. Simmer for 5 to 7 minutes.
5. Cool completely. Add the saffron mixture and cardamom powder and mix well.
6. Pour into shallow freezer proof containers and freeze till slushy (approx. 3 to 4 hours).

7. Remove and blend in a liquidiser to break all the ice crystals till the mixture is smooth and creamy.
8. Pour into 6 kulfi moulds and freeze overnight until it sets.
9. To unmould, allow the moulds to remain outside the refrigerator for 5 minutes and then unmould by inserting a wooden skewer stick or a fork in the centre of the kulfi and pulling it out.

Serve topped with the strawberry sauce.

Nutritive values per serving :

AMT	ENERGY	PROTEIN	CHO	FAT	VIT.A	VIT.C	CALCIUM	IRON	F.ACID	FIBRE
gm	kcal	gm	gm	gm	mcg	mg	mg	mg	mcg	gm
38	99	6.5	18.2	0.0	2.5	7.4	232.2	0.5	0.0	0.2

Gajar Halwa

Picture on page 76

Preparation time :
5 minutes.
Cooking time :
15 minutes.
Serves *5.*

Everyone loves to savour the traditional flavours of home-made mithais. Here's an easy way to make tasty gajar halwa that is low on calories and yet satisfies your sweet tooth. Packed with fresh carrots, this classic recipe provides you plenty of vitamin A which helps to maintain a healthy vision and glowing skin.

2 cups carrots, grated
2 cups low fat milk, page 142
6 tablespoons low fat milk powder
4 teaspoons sugar
½ teaspoon cardamom (elaichi) powder

1. Combine the carrots with the milk and pressure cook for 2 whistles.
2. Add the milk powder, sugar and cardamom powder and cook for 3 to 4 minutes, while stirring continuously.
   Serve hot.

Nutritive values per serving :

AMT	ENERGY	PROTEIN	CHO	FAT	VIT.A	VIT.C	CALCIUM	IRON	F.ACID	FIBRE
gm	kcal	gm	gm	gm	mcg	mg	mg	mg	mcg	gm
62	113	8.8	19.1	0.1	665.3	2.2	335.0	0.7	5.3	0.4

Sweet Potato Puranpoli

Preparation time :
10 minutes.
Cooking time :
10 minutes.
Makes 4 puranpolis.

A healthy version of the traditional calorie laden puranpolis. Sweet potatoes have been used instead of dal to minimize the sugar used. Cardamom powder, nutmeg and saffron add to the pleasing aroma of these fat-free puranpolis.
Enjoy them with low fat milk instead of ghee for a sweet ending!

For the dough

1/3 cup whole wheat flour (gehun ka atta)
4 tablespoons low fat milk, page 142

To be mixed into a filling

1/2 cup boiled and grated sweet potato
4 teaspoons sugar
1/8 teaspoon nutmeg (jaiphal) powder
1/8 teaspoon cardamom (elaichi) powder
a few saffron strands

For the dough

1. Make a soft dough using the flour and milk and knead well.
2. Divide the dough into 4 equal portions and keep aside.

How to proceed

1. Roll out one portion of the dough into a circle of 75 mm. (3") diameter.
2. Place one portion of the filling mixture in the centre of the circle.
3. Bring together all the sides in the centre and seal tightly.
4. Roll out again into a circle of 125 mm. (5") diameter using flour to roll.
5. Cook on a non-stick pan until both sides are brown.
6. Repeat with the remaining dough and filling to make 3 more puranpolis. Serve hot.

Nutritive values per puranpoli :

AMT	ENERGY	PROTEIN	CHO	FAT	VIT.A	VIT.C	CALCIUM	IRON	F.ACID	FIBRE
gm	kcal	gm	gm	gm	mcg	mg	mg	mg	mcg	gm
28	70	1.8	15.4	0.2	3.3	3.0	30.4	0.5	3.2	0.3

Basic Recipes

Low Fat Milk

Preparation time :
5 minutes.
Cooking time :
7 minutes.
Makes *1 litre (5 cups).*

This low fat milk has been made using skim milk powder and is virtually fat free and has all the goodness of milk like protein, calcium and vitamin B_2. Skim milk powder is easily available at all leading grocery stores. Alternatively, feel free to use 99% fat free milk (low fat milk) readily available in tetrapacks in the market.

This low fat milk gives you only 71 calories per cup as compared to 234 calories per cup along with 13 grams of fat from full fat milk. So start using low fat milk to prepare milkshakes, desserts and for virtually any recipe where milk is required.

100 grams skim milk powder
1 litre water

1. Mix the skim milk powder in 1½ cups of water and make a smooth paste.
2. Add the remaining water and mix well using a whisk.
3. Boil and use as required.

Handy Tip *Different packets of skim milk have different methods of preparation. The above procedure has been given for your guidance but please follow the instructions on the packet you use.*

Nutritive values per cup (200 ml) :

AMT	ENERGY	PROTEIN	CHO	FAT	VIT.A	VIT.C	CALCIUM	IRON	F.ACID	FIBRE
ml	kcal	gm	gm	gm	mcg	mg	mg	mg	mcg	gm
200	71	7.6	10.2	0.0	0.0	1.0	274.0	0.3	0.0	0.0

Low Fat Curds

Preparation time :
5 minutes.
Setting time :
6 hours.
Makes 5 cups.

Curds are a nutritious addition to your diet. They are easier to digest than milk and when accompanied with dishes like parathas, biryanis etc., curds complement the protein present in cereals and make it a complete protein.
Use this low fat version of curds as an accompaniment to a main meal or in raitas, salad dressings etc. to enjoy a delightful low calorie fare.

1 litre low fat milk, page 142
1 tablespoon curds (made the previous day)

1. Warm the milk.
2. Add the curds, mix well and cover.
3. Keep aside until the curds set (approx. 5 to 6 hours). During the cold climate, place inside a cupboard or a closed oven for setting.

Nutritive values per cup (200 ml) :

AMT	ENERGY	PROTEIN	CHO	FAT	VIT.A	VIT.C	CALCIUM	IRON	F.ACID	FIBRE
ml	kcal	gm	gm	gm	mcg	mg	mg	mg	mcg	gm
200	71	7.6	10.2	0.0	0.0	1.0	274.0	0.3	0.0	0.0

Low Fat Paneer

Preparation time :
30 minutes.

Cooking time :
10 minutes.

Makes *100 grams. (approx. ¾ cup).*

The low calorie paneer is a great recipe for weight watchers which can be easily incorporated into vegetables (subjis) and snacks. This paneer is made from skim milk which has all the goodness of milk and only 0.1 grams of fat as compared to 23 grams of fat in full fat paneer. For milk fussy adults, it is a superb way of increasing the intake of protein (necessary for maintenance of body cells) and calcium (required for healthy bones).

2 cups low fat milk, page 142
1 cup low fat curds, page 143, beaten

1. Put the milk to boil in a broad pan. When it starts boiling, add the low fat curds and mix well.
2. Remove from the heat and stir gently until the milk curdles.
3. Strain the curdled milk in a muslin cloth and hang for about ½ hour to allow the whey to drain out.
   Use as required.

Handy Tip *If the milk has not curdled completely in step 2, cook the mixture a little longer.*

Nutritive values per 100 grams (approx. ¾ cup) :

AMT	ENERGY	PROTEIN	CHO	FAT	VIT.A	VIT.C	CALCIUM	IRON	F.ACID	FIBRE
gm	kcal	gm	gm	gm	mcg	mg	mg	mg	mcg	gm
100	214	22.8	30.6	0.1	0.0	3.0	822.0	0.8	0.0	0.0

Low Calorie Green Chutney

Preparation time :
10 minutes.
Cooking time :
2 minutes.
Makes *½ cup.*
(approx. 7 tablespoons).

Chutneys are a favourite accompaniment for snacks as well for main meals. This low calorie chutney uses roasted chana dal (daria) instead of fat-laden ingredients like coconut and peanuts. Curds have been used to retain the fresh green colour of this chutney.
It can be stored if refrigerated for 2 to 3 days.

½ cup roasted chana dal (daria)
¼ cup chopped coriander
1 green chilli, chopped
1 tablespoon low fat curds, page 143, beaten
salt to taste

For the seasoning

½ teaspoon oil
a pinch of asafoetida (hing)
⅛ teaspoon mustard seeds (rai)

1. Combine the chana dal, coriander and green chilli with 1 cup of water and grind to a smooth paste.
2. For the seasoning, heat the oil in a non-stick pan and add the asafoetida and mustard seeds and fry until the seeds crackle.
3. Pour the seasoning over the chutney, add the curds and mix well.

Nutritive values per tablespoon :

AMT	ENERGY	PROTEIN	CHO	FAT	VIT.A	VIT.C	CALCIUM	IRON	F.ACID	FIBRE
gm	kcal	gm	gm	gm	mcg	mg	mg	mg	mcg	gm
13	46	2.5	7.2	0.8	76.0	1.3	11.1	0.6	17.3	0.2

Tomato Chutney

Preparation time :
10 minutes.
Cooking time :
10 minutes.
Makes ¾ cup.
(approx. 10 tablespoons)

Like most South Indian recipes, this is a hot and spicy tomato and onion chutney. Perk up your meal with this recipe. Purée this to make a coarse chutney and enjoy the contrasting flavours.

1 cup tomato, chopped
¼ cup onions, chopped
2 green chillies, chopped
½ teaspoon split Bengal gram (chana dal)
½ teaspoon urad dal (split black lentils)
8 to 10 curry leaves
¼ teaspoon turmeric powder (haldi)
1 teaspoon oil
salt to taste

1. Heat the oil in a non-stick pan, add the green chillies, chana dal, urad dal and curry leaves and sauté for a few seconds.
2. Add the onions and sauté till they turn translucent.
3. Add the chopped tomato, turmeric powder and salt and sauté for another 4 to 5 minutes.
4. Allow to cool completely.
5. Purée the mixture for a few seconds in a blender to get a coarse chunky chutney.

   Serve at room temperature or store upto 2 days refrigerated.

Nutritive values per tablespoon :

AMT	ENERGY	PROTEIN	CHO	FAT	VIT.A	VIT.C	CALCIUM	IRON	F.ACID	FIBRE
gm	kcal	gm	gm	gm	mcg	mg	mg	mg	mcg	gm
20	11	0.3	1.2	0.6	59.7	4.6	9.5	0.1	5.6	0.2

Mint and Coriander Chutney

Preparation time :
10 minutes.

No Cooking.

Makes *1 cup.*
(approx. 14 tablespoons).

A mint and coriander flavoured chutney which is great for sandwich spreads. Lemon juice enhances the flavours of mint and coriander and prevents discoloration of the greens.
This green chutney is probably the most favourite Indian accompaniment. Chilas, tikkis, dhoklas etc. are considered incomplete without this chutney.

2 cups chopped mint (phudina) leaves
1 cup chopped coriander
1 large onion, sliced
juice of 1 to 2 lemons
1 teaspoon sugar
4 to 6 green chillies
salt to taste

1. Combine all the ingredients and grind to a smooth paste in a blender using very little water.
2. Refrigerate and use as required.

Nutritive values per tablespoon :

AMT	ENERGY	PROTEIN	CHO	FAT	VIT.A	VIT.C	CALCIUM	IRON	F.ACID	FIBRE
gm	kcal	gm	gm	gm	mcg	mg	mg	mg	mcg	gm
16	10	0.4	1.9	0.1	193.0	5.2	16.7	0.7	5.3	0.2

Major Nutrients and their Sources

Nutrients and their Functions	Food Sources
CARBOHYDRATES (1 gm. of carbohydrates = 4 calories) ✔ Extremely necessary to provide energy to your body	✔ Cereals like whole wheat, jowar, bajra, barley, buckwheat, corn, ragi (nachni) etc. ✔ Pulses and legumes like rajma, moong, cow pea (chawli) etc. ✔ Vegetables like potato, yam (suran), sweet potato etc.* ✔ Fruits like banana, chickoo etc.* ✔ Sugar, jaggery, honey etc.*
PROTEIN (1gm. of protein = 4 calories) ✔ Repair and maintenance of body tissues	✔ Pulses and legumes like chana dal, rajma, toovar (arhar) dal, moath beans (matki) etc. ✔ Low fat dairy products like milk, curds, paneer etc. ✔ Soyabean and its products like tofu, soya nuggets, soyamilk etc.
FIBRE ✔ Provides roughage and adds bulk to your diet ✔ Keeps you satiated for longer periods of time and prevents bingeing on high calorie snacks	✔ Cereals like brown rice, whole wheat, wheat bran, oats, barley, jowar, buckwheat, bajra, ragi (nachni) etc. ✔ Pulses and legumes like rajma, soyabean etc. ✔ Vegetables like green peas, drumsticks, cluster beans (gavarfali) etc. ✔ Fruits like orange, sweet lime, guava etc.
VITAMINS **1. Vitamin A** ✔ To maintain a normal vision ✔ Required for maintenance of healthy skin ✔ Increases immunity and protects from diseases like coughs, colds, influenza, etc.	✔ Dark green leafy vegetables like spinach (palak), fenugreek (methi), cow pea (chawli) leaves etc. ✔ Yellow orange fruits and vegetables like orange, carrot, red pumpkin, tomato, papaya etc. ✔ Low fat dairy products like milk, paneer, curds etc.
2. Vitamin B_1 (Thiamin) ✔ Aids in the metabolism of energy in your body	✔ Cereals like whole wheat, wheat bran, rice, jowar etc. ✔ Dark green leafy vegetables like fenugreek (methi), spinach (palak) etc.

* *Foods to be eaten in restricted amounts. For a detailed list of foods to be restricted refer to page 155.*

Nutrients and their Functions	Food Sources
3. Vitamin B_2 (Riboflavin) ✔ Aids in the metabolism of energy and protein in your body ✔ Promotes healthy skin	✔ Low fat dairy products like milk, curds, paneer etc. ✔ Dark green leafy vegetables like cow pea (chawli) leaves, spinach (palak) etc. ✔ Cereals like whole wheat, rice, bajra etc. ✔ Pulses and legumes like moong dal, rajma, soyabean etc.
4. Vitamin B_3 (Niacin) ✔ Aids in the metabolism of energy, protein, carbohydrate and fat in your body	✔ Cereals like barley, whole wheat, rice bran etc. ✔ Pulses and legumes like chana dal, soyabean, moong etc.
5. Vitamin B_6 (Pyridoxine) ✔ Helps in the breakdown of protein and fat in your body	✔ Cereals like whole wheat, wheat bran, brown rice, broken wheat (dalia), oats, buckwheat, barley etc.
6. Vitamin B_{12} (Cyanocobalamin) ✔ Required for proper functioning of cells in your body	✔ Soyabean and its products like soya nuggets, tofu etc. are the only vegetarian sources of this vitamin.
7. Folic Acid ✔ Helps in the formation and multiplication of red blood cells in your body	✔ Vegetables like cluster beans (gavarfali), spinach (palak), green peas, broccoli, beetroot, ladies finger (bhindi), potato* etc. ✔ Bajra and soyabean
8. Vitamin C (Ascorbic acid) ✔ Strengthens your immunity and protects you from infections ✔ Aids in the absorption of iron present in your food ✔ Maintenance of teeth, skin, muscles and bones	✔ Citrus fruits like orange, guava, lemon, sweet lime etc. ✔ Other fruits like amla and papaya ✔ Vegetables like broccoli, capsicum and cabbage
9. Vitamin D ✔ Aids in the absorption of calcium in your body which in turn makes your bones healthy	✔ Is naturally produced by your body in the presence of sunlight ✔ Low fat dairy products like milk, curds, paneer etc.
10. Vitamin E ✔ Essential for maintaining healthy body cells	✔ All vegetable oils ✔ Cereals like wheat germ, bajra, jowar etc.
11. Vitamin K ✔ Helps in clotting your blood during injuries	✔ Vegetables like cauliflower, tomato, spinach (palak) etc. ✔ Soyabean

* *Foods to be eaten in restricted amounts. For a detailed list of foods to be restricted refer to page 155.*

Nutrients and their Functions	Food Sources
MINERALS **1. Calcium and Phosphorus** ✔ Strengthening of bones and teeth	✔ Low fat dairy products like milk, curds, paneer etc. ✔ Vegetables like broccoli, spinach (palak), fenugreek (methi) etc. ✔ Soyabean and its products like tofu, soya nuggets etc. ✔ Ragi (nachni)
2. Iron ✔ Production of red blood cells ✔ Essential to supply oxygen to your body cells	✔ Dark green leafy vegetables like spinach (palak), cow pea (chawli) leaves, fenugreek (methi) etc. ✔ Cereals and pulses like bajra, cow pea (chawli), dry peas etc. ✔ Jaggery*
3. Sodium ✔ Maintenance of fluid balance in your body ✔ Maintenance of muscle and nerve activity	✔ Salt ✔ Low fat dairy products like milk, curds, paneer etc. ✔ Vegetables like spinach (palak), celery etc. ✔ Cereals and legumes
4. Potassium ✔ Maintenance of fluid balance in the body ✔ Maintenance of muscle and nerve activity	✔ Low fat dairy produts like milk, curds, paneer etc. ✔ Vegetables like potato*, tomato, carrot, celery etc. ✔ Fruits like orange, grapes* etc.
5. Iodine ✔ Proper functioning of the thyroid gland	✔ Iodized salt ✔ Low fat dairy products like milk, curds, paneer etc.
6. Copper ✔ Essential for the formation of haemoglobin and melanin (skin pigment) in your body ✔ A component of many enzymes in your body	✔ Whole cereals and pulses like bajra, barley, chana, masoor etc.
7. Magnesium ✔ Aids in the metabolism of carbohydrates by activating certain enzymes ✔ Constituent of bones and muscles	✔ Low fat dairy products like milk, curds, paneer, etc. ✔ Pulses and legumes like moath beans (matki), soyabean, rajma etc. ✔ Vegetables like spinach (palak), celery etc.
8. Zinc ✔ Normal functioning of the brain ✔ Promotes growth of body tissues and cells	✔ Low fat dairy products like milk, paneer, curds etc. ✔ Cereals like bajra, ragi (nachni), whole wheat, wheat germ etc. ✔ Pulses and legumes like chana dal, cow pea (chawli), soyabean etc.

* *Foods to be eaten in restricted amounts. For a detailed list of foods to be restricted refer to page 155.*

Food Allowed, Restricted and Forbidden for Weight Watchers

For a healthy and sustained weight loss, you need a balanced and varied diet that will cut calories to a safe level without sacrificing essential nutrients and one that will encourage healthy eating habits which stay with you for a life time.

Foods Allowed

Given below is the list of foods that can be eaten when you are on a weight loss programme. All values are given per standard cup (200 ml) measures and arranged in the increasing order of their energy values.

	Energy kcal	Protein gm	CHO gm	Fat gm	Fibre gm
Cereals					
Puffed rice (mumara)	46	1.1	10.3	6.0	0.0
Makai ka atta	118	4.4	23.1	0.8	1.8
Poha (beaten rice flakes)	208	4.0	46.4	0.7	0.4
Quick rolled oats	277	10.1	46.5	5.6	2.6
Jowar flour (white millet flour)	342	10.2	71.1	1.9	9.8
Bajra flour (black millet flour)	347	11.1	64.8	2.5	1.2
Whole wheat flour (gehun ka atta)	368	13.1	75.0	1.8	1.9
Ragi (nachni) flour	374	8.3	82.1	1.5	4.1
Buckwheat (kutto or kutti no daro)	452	14.4	91.1	3.4	12.0
Barley (jau)	470	16.0	97.4	1.8	5.5
Broken wheat (dalia)	527	12.1	114.3	2.4	2.5
Rice	552	10.9	125.1	0.8	0.3
Pulses and Legumes					
Moong sprouts	180	13.0	30.6	0.7	2.2
Matki (moath beans) sprouts	188	13.5	32.2	0.6	2.6
Soyabean flour	294	29.4	14.2	13.3	2.5
Bengal gram flour (besan)	305	17.1	49.0	4.6	1.0
Black eyed beans (lobhia)	517	42.2	94.7	1.8	7.5
Rajma (kidney beans)	519	35.7	90.9	2.0	7.2
Masoor dal (split red lentils)	521	38.2	89.7	1.1	1.1
Urad dal (split black lentils)	524	36.2	90.0	2.1	1.4
Moong (whole green gram)	541	38.9	91.9	2.1	6.6
Matki (moath beans)	548	39.2	93.8	1.8	7.5
Toovar (arhar) dal	549	36.6	94.5	2.8	2.5
Masoor (whole red lentils)	556	40.7	95.6	1.1	1.1
Vaal (field beans)	562	40.3	97.4	1.3	2.3
Chick peas (kabuli chana)	590	28.0	99.9	8.7	6.4
Chana dal (split Bengal gram)	590	28.0	99.9	8.7	6.4
Moong dal (split yellow gram)	606	42.6	104.2	2.1	1.4

Foods Allowed

Given below is the list of foods that can be eaten when you are on a weight loss programme. All values are given per standard cup (200 ml) measures and arranged in the increasing order of their energy values.

	Energy kcal	Protein gm	CHO gm	Fat gm	Fibre gm
Vegetables					
Leafy Vegetables					
Coriander, chopped	11	0.8	1.6	0.2	0.6
Fenugreek (methi), chopped	14	1.2	1.7	0.3	0.3
Mint (phudina), chopped	14	1.4	1.7	0.2	0.6
Spinach (palak), chopped	18	1.4	0.5	0.5	0.4
Cabbage/ Red cabbage, shredded	22	1.5	3.8	0.1	1.2
Chawli (cow pea) leaves, chopped	26	2.3	2.8	0.5	0.8
Lettuce, torn	34	3.4	4.0	0.5	0.8
Other Vegetables					
Bottle gourd (lauki/doodhi), chopped	13	0.2	2.7	0.1	0.6
Turai (ridge gourd), chopped	15	0.4	2.9	0.1	0.4
Cucumber, chopped	16	0.5	3.1	0.1	0.5
Cluster beans (gavarfali), chopped	16	3.2	1.6	0.4	3.2
Mushrooms, chopped	19	1.5	3.4	0.3	1.0
Radish (mooli), chopped	20	0.8	4.0	0.1	0.9
Celery stalks, chopped	20	3.9	0.9	0.1	1.3
Cauliflower, florets	22	1.9	3.0	0.3	0.9
Bhindi (ladies fingers), chopped	25	1.3	4.5	0.1	0.8
French beans, chopped	26	1.7	4.5	0.1	1.8
Tendli, chopped	26	4.2	3.3	0.2	1.2
Carrot, chopped	27	0.5	5.9	0.1	0.7
Karela (bitter gourd), chopped	28	1.8	4.7	0.2	0.9
Capsicum (red, yellow and green), chopped	29	1.6	5.2	0.4	1.2
Brinjals (baingan), chopped	30	1.8	5.0	0.4	1.6
Tomato, chopped	31	1.4	0.3	0.3	1.2
Beetroot, chopped	32	1.3	6.5	0.1	0.7
Red pumpkin (kaddu), chopped	32	1.8	5.8	0.1	0.9
Spring onions (including greens), chopped	32	0.8	7.1	0.1	0.4
Drumsticks, chopped	42	4.0	5.9	0.2	6.9
Onions, chopped	66	1.6	14.7	0.1	0.8
Baby corn	122	4.4	30.6	0.1	3.1
Sweet corn	122	4.4	30.6	0.1	3.1
Green peas	130	10.1	22.3	0.1	5.6

Foods Allowed

Given below is the list of foods that can be eaten when you are on a weight loss programme. All values are given per standard cup (200 ml) measures and arranged in the increasing order of their energy values.

	Energy kcal	Protein gm	CHO gm	Fat gm	Fibre gm
Fruits					
Watermelon (tarbuj), chopped	25	0.0	5.0	0.0	0.0
Muskmelon (kharbooja), chopped	26	0.5	5.3	0.3	0.6
Papaya, chopped	45	0.8	10.1	0.1	1.1
Guava, chopped	66	1.2	14.6	0.4	6.8
Strawberry, quartered	66	1.1	14.7	0.3	1.7
Apple, chopped	68	0.2	15.5	0.6	1.2
Lychee, chopped	68	1.2	15.2	0.2	0.5
Pears, chopped	71	0.8	16.2	0.3	1.4
Plums, sliced	73	1.0	15.5	0.7	0.6
Pineapple, chopped	76	0.7	17.9	0.2	0.8
Sweet lime, segmented	76	1.4	16.4	0.5	0.9
Peaches, chopped	76	1.7	14.7	0.6	1.7
Orange, segmented	84	1.2	19.2	10.4	0.5
Pomegranate (anar)	94	2.3	20.9	0.1	7.3
Cherry, chopped	110	1.9	23.7	0.9	0.7
Black jamun, chopped	124	1.4	28.0	0.6	0.3
Dairy Products					
Low fat milk	71	7.6	10.2	0.0	0.0
Low fat curds	71	7.6	10.2	0.0	0.0
Low fat paneer, chopped	174	15.6	27.6	0.6	0.0

Foods Restricted

Given below is the list of foods which you can occasionally eat when you are on a weight loss programme. All values are given for standard cup (200 ml) measures and arranged in the increasing order of their energy values.

	Energy kcal	Protein gm	CHO gm	Fat gm	Fibre gm
Vegetables (for a standard 200 ml cup)					
Potato, chopped	89	1.5	20.8	0.1	0.4
Suran (yam), chopped	101	1.5	23.6	0.1	0.6
Kand (purple yam), chopped	142	1.8	33.3	0.1	1.0
Sweet potato, chopped	170	1.7	40.0	0.4	1.1
Fruits (for a standard 200 ml cup)					
Grapes	99	0.7	23.1	0.4	4.1
Mango, chopped	104	0.9	23.7	1.4	3.4
Chickoo, chopped	127	0.9	27.8	1.4	3.4
Custard apple, chopped	187	2.9	42.3	0.7	1.6
Banana, chopped	348	3.6	81.6	0.9	1.2
Sugars (for 1 teaspoon)					
Sugar	20	0.0	5.0	0.0	0.0
Honey	21	0.6	5.8	0.0	0.0
Jaggery	23	0.0	5.7	0.0	0.0
Fats (for 1 teaspoon)					
Oil	45	0.0	0.0	5.0	0.0
Nuts and Oilseeds (for 1 teaspoon)					
Dates	4	0.0	0.1	0.0	0.1
Raisins/ sultanas	6	0.1	1.5	0.0	0.0

Foods Forbidden

Given below is the list of foods which you need to avoid when you are on a weight loss programme. All values are given for standard cup (200 ml) measures and arranged in the increasing order of their energy values.

	Energy kcal	Protein gm	CHO gm	Fat gm	Fibre gm
Cereals (for a standard 200 ml cup)					
Plain flour (maida)	383	12.1	81.3	1.0	0.3
Semolina (rawa)	487	14.6	104.7	1.1	0.3
Dairy products (for a standard 200 ml cup)					
Full fat milk	234	8.6	10.0	9.3	0.0
Full fat paneer, chopped	420	19.0	11.4	33.1	0.0
Full fat cheese, chopped	536	37.1	9.7	38.7	0.0
Cream	582	4.0	5.6	60.8	0.0
Full fat khoya (mava)	595	35.9	28.8	37.8	0.0
Fats (for 1 teaspoon)					
Butter	36	0.0	0.0	4.9	0.0
Ghee	45	0.0	0.0	5.0	0.0
Nuts and Oilseeds (for 1 teaspoon)					
Sesame seeds (til)	11	0.4	0.5	0.9	0.2
Cashewnuts	15	0.5	0.6	1.2	0.2
Almonds	16	0.5	0.3	1.5	0.0
Pistachios	19	0.6	0.5	1.6	0.1
Dry coconut (kopra), grated	20	0.2	0.6	1.9	0.2
Walnuts	21	0.5	0.3	1.9	0.1
Fresh coconut, grated	22	0.2	0.7	2.1	0.0
Peanuts	28	1.3	1.3	2.0	0.2

Menu Planner

As you gather knowledge about your dietary requirements and enjoy cooking the recipes from this book, you'll find these nutritonally balanced menus make your daily selection much easier. Ideally, the day should begin with a low fat, energy boosting breakfast, the main meal should be taken at lunchtime, supplemented by snacks in the evening and the final meal of the day should be relatively light. Begin following these menus and you'll realize healthy eating has real benefits—you'll have more energy, improved resistance to disease and of course lose weight too.

1st Menu

Meal	Menu	Amount	Energy kcal	Protein gm	CHO gm	Fat gm	Fibre gm
Breakfast	High Fibre Chilas, page 32	2 nos.	188	5.5	33.6	3.6	4.1
	Mint and Coriander Chutney, page 147	2 tablespoons	20	0.8	3.8	0.2	0.4
	Grape Lassi, page 40	1 glass	105	4.2	21.6	0.2	2.0
			313	**10.5**	**59.0**	**4.0**	**6.5**
Lunch	Dhan-saak Dal, page 95	1 serving	127	7.2	20.5	1.8	0.8
	Brown Rice, page 104	1 serving	235	4.4	50.8	1.6	0.3
	Spicy Kachumber, page 125	1 serving	16	0.5	3 3	0.1	0.4
	Gajar Halwa, page 138	1 serving	113	8.8	19.1	0.1	0.4
			491	**20.9**	**93.7**	**3.6**	**1.9**
Evening Snack	Vegetable Corn Bake, page 30	1 serving	203	7.6	36.5	2.9	1.6
	Apple	1 no.	124	0.4	28.1	1.1	2.1
			327	**8.0**	**64.6**	**4.0**	**3.7**
Dinner	Methi Paneer Parathas, page 115	2 nos.	218	10.9	36.2	3.3	0.8
	Tamatar ki Kadhi, page 87	1 serving	46	1.2	6.9	1.5	0.7
	Moong Dal Seekh Kebabs, page 42	3 nos.	92	4.9	14.7	1.5	0.3
			356	**17.0**	**57.8**	**6.3**	**1.8**
Total			**1487**	**56.4**	**275.1**	**17.9**	**13.9**

2nd Menu

Meal	Menu	Amount	Energy kcal	Protein gm	CHO gm	Fat gm	Fibre gm
Breakfast	Muesli, page 24	1 serving	281	13.2	51.6	2.3	2.6
			281	**13.2**	**51.6**	**2.3**	**2.6**
Lunch	Phulka	2 nos.	102	3.6	20.8	0.5	0.6
	Healthy Oondhiya, page74	1 serving	197	5.2	40.6	1.6	1.9
	Sweet Lime and Pepper Salad, page 129	1 serving	68	3.5	12.0	0.7	1.6
	Spicy Sprouts Pulao, page 105	1 serving	216	6.4	43.1	2.0	0.9
			583	**18.7**	**116.5**	**4.8**	**4.8**
Evening Snack	Paneer Tikka Kathi Rolls, page 53	2 nos.	162	10.0	26.9	1.6	0.7
	Mint and Coriander Chutney, page 147	2 tablespoons	20	0.8	3.8	0.2	0.4
	Pineapple	1 cup	76	0.7	17.9	0.2	0.8
			258	**11.5**	**48.6**	**2.0**	**1.9**
Dinner	Palak aur Chawal ki Röti, page 111	4 nos.	190	4.86	41.3	0.7	0.4
	Turai aur Moong ki Dal, page 92	1 serving	56	2.7	8.2	1.4	0.4
	Minty Bean Salad, page 125	1 serving	53	3.1	9.6	0.2	0.9
	Tandoori Mushrooms, page 47	1 serving	40	2.6	5.1	1.6	1.0
	Low Fat Curds, page 145	¼ cup	18	1.9	2.6	0.0	0.0
			357	**14.9**	**66.8**	**3.9**	**2.7**
Total			**1479**	**58.3**	**283.5**	**13.0**	**12.0**

3rd Menu

Meal	Menu	Amount	Energy kcal	Protein gm	CHO gm	Fat gm	Fibre gm
Breakfast	Protein Packed Poha, page 27	1 serving	156	4.8	30.3	3.1	1.1
	Date and Apple Shake, page 36	1 glass	120	7.9	21.5	0.3	1.0
			276	**12.7**	**51.8**	**3.4**	**2.1**
Lunch	Masala Bhaat, page 100	1 serving	169	3.7	35.2	1.6	0.6
	Doodhi Theplas, page 117	3 nos.	165	6.0	31.4	1.8	0.9
	Vaal ki Usal, page 81	1 serving	187	10.6	32.5	1.6	0.8
	Mixed Veggie Raita, page 130	1 serving	29	2.4	4.8	0.1	0.4
			550	**22.7**	**103.9**	**5.1**	**2.7**
Evening Snack	Green Pea Pankis, page 48	4 nos.	75	2.4	12.7	1.6	0.5
	Low Calorie Green Chutney, page 145	2 tablespoons	92	5.0	14.2	1.6	0.4
	Melon Tango, page 38	1 serving	89	2.2	19.1	0.4	0.6
			256	**9.6**	**46.0**	**3.6**	**1.5**
Dinner	Methi Makai ki Roti, page 110	4 nos.	154	4.8	24.3	4.2	0.8
	Dal Makhani, page 80	1 serving	134	8.6	21.1	1.7	0.8
	Bharva Baingan, page 71	1 serving	59	1.5	9.8	1.5	0.6
	Barley and Corn Kachumber, page 121	1 serving	53	1.9	10.8	0.3	1.0
			400	**16.8**	**66.0**	**7.7**	**3.2**
Total			**1482**	**61.8**	**267.7**	**19.8**	**9.5**

4th Menu

Meal	Menu	Amount	Energy kcal	Protein gm	CHO gm	Fat gm	Fibre gm
Breakfast	Nutritious Stuffed Idlis, page 25	2 nos.	131	4.0	26.6	0.9	0.8
	Sambhar, page 93	1 serving	146	8.3	24.8	1.5	0.9
	Orange	1 no.	51	0.7	11.6	0.2	0.3
			328	**13.0**	**63.0**	**2.6**	**2.0**
Lunch	Nutritious Garlic Naans, page 113	2 nos.	126	5.6	20.3	2.5	0.7
	Hariyali Dal, page 86	1 serving	117	6.0	17.0	2.8	0.7
	Vegetable Biryani, page 98	1 serving	251	8.5	47.5	2.9	1.4
	Lauki aur Phudine ka Raita, page 120	1 serving	25	2.1	4.0	0.1	0.2
			519	**22.2**	**88.8**	**8.3**	**3.0**
Evening Snack	Lapsi Methi Muthias, page 49	1 serving	110	2.7	20.3	2.0	0.4
	Pineapple Celery Juice, page 39	1 glass	79	0.8	18.3	0.2	1.0
			256	**46.0**	**9.6**	**3.6**	**1.5**
Dinner	Saatdhan Parathas, page 112	4 nos.	224	7.2	41.0	3.5	1.3
	Radish Koftas in Kadhi, page 84	1 serving	86	5.6	12.2	1.7	0.2
	Pineapple Cucumber Salad, page 123	1 serving	69	2.4	13.5	0.7	1.0
	Low Fat Kulfi with Strawberry Sauce, page 136	1 serving	99	6.5	18.2	0.0	0.1
			478	**21.7**	**84.9**	**5.9**	**2.6**
Total			**1514**	**60.4**	**275.3**	**19.0**	**9.0**